# ORIGINS AND GROWTH OF SOCIOLOGICAL THEORY

*Readings on the History of Sociology*

*edited by*
## Antonio O. Donini
*and*
## Joseph A. Novack

Nelson-Hall nh Chicago

Library of Congress Cataloging in Publication Data

Main entry under title:

Origins and growth of sociological theory.

Includes bibliographical references and index.
1. Sociology — History.   I. Donini, Antonio O.
II. Novack, Joseph A.
HM19.869          301'.09       81-22322
ISBN 0-88229-614-0 (cloth)          AACR2
ISBN 0-88229-801-0 (paper)

Manufactured in the United States of America

10   9   8   7   6   5   4   3   2   1

The paper in this book is pH neutral (acid-free).

# CONTENTS

# 1
# Introduction: From Social Philosophy to Sociological Theory

This volume represents a brief summary and a critical analysis of the growth of sociological thought and the emergence of sociology from social philosophy.

Social theorists — both philosophers and sociologists — have contributed to this historical development. Sociology, then, is the result of a gradual evolution of thought in the western hemisphere, proceeding from theological or religious thinking, through philosophical or analytic reasoning, to positive or empirical science.

Philosophy was viewed as man's intellectual attempt to explain the totality of reality. Therefore, an emphasis can be found in social philosophy upon an organizing or central metaphysical principle.

Traditional philosophical theories of society use the *deductive method*. Their principles and conclusions are not empirically verifiable. These theories deal with normative aspects rather than with factual aspects of social reality, i.e., with how society should be, or ought to be, not with how society actually is. On the other side, sociological theories of society use the *inductive method*. As with any other empirical science, they start with observation or experimentation of verifiable phenomena. Consequently, sociological theories of society deal with social reality and its interpretation.

Social theories, either philosophical or sociological, grow out of specific crises writers observe or experience in their societies. They try to find an explanation for and/or a solution to the problems of their time. Therefore, social theories should be discussed and analyzed within the personal, social, and historical context of the writer under consideration. Moreover, contemporary sociological theories are strongly affected by the so-called "classic social theories."

With this assumption in mind, we begin our discussion of the develop-

1

ment of sociological thought with a review of the main ideas advanced by some of the most important social philosophers of the late seventeenth through the nineteenth centuries. In fact, it was only during the late nineteenth century that social philosophy gradually differentiated into sociology.

Even though *systematic sociology* begins with Auguste Comte, nevertheless "there was plenty of *sociological thinking* before Comte." In other terms, sociological theory begins only when the science of society became differentiated from social philosophy. It could only occur when the development in positive knowledge and empirical methods made possible an "empirical science" of social phenomena. Since then, sociological theories — even though limited by different philosophical assumptions — should be, in principle, empirically verifiable. Philosophy is used as an analytical tool at the explanatory level of inquiry. It is worth mentioning also, that in the actual practice of social scientists the line between the two disciplines is not always clearly drawn.

We do not agree with those who believe that sociology could never exist if there had been no Auguste Comte. Actually, there is a general agreement today that Saint-Simon and many other social thinkers have anticipated most of the theoretical and sociological views of Comte. Moreover, Comte's most valid contribution to the science of society is the systematic integration of the social theories which were currently held in his day, such as those of Vico, Montesquieu, Hume, Condorcet, Saint-Simon, and many others.

Sociological theory can be defined as a systematic attempt to explain scientifically social interaction. Timasheff has listed some of the concerns of sociological theory, both past and present. The problems addressed can be indicated by a series of questions:

What is society and culture?

What are the basic units into which society and culture should be analyzed?

What is the relationship between society, culture, and personality?

What are the factors determining the state of a society and a culture, or change in a society or culture?

What is sociology and what are its appropriate methods?[1]

As might be imagined, the answers that have developed for these questions have been many and diverse. These are, in fact, "answers" that have been derived from different theoretical perspectives.

Because social philosophy is a much older discipline than sociology and because modern sociology has been built, in part, upon that older discipline it is difficult to assess at which historical point a discussion of the two should begin. In one sense it would be possible to go back into antiquity and dwell upon those earlier philosophical efforts at great length. However, the purpose of this book is to provide the student with a general overview of the development of sociology, not a detailed analysis of all social philosophies. The focal point of this book rests upon the time frame that extends from the seventeenth century to the present. It is of value to the student, however, to be aware of the philosophical efforts that predate our time frame.

Although the proposed time frame of this work is the latter part of the seventeenth century to the present, one historical exception is needed. The writings of Ibn Khaldun (1332–1406) are such that from the point of view of sociological sophistication they are distinctly relevant to our discussion. Khaldun, a fourteenth-century Arab, applied a systematic scheme of analysis to the study of social phenomena.

In his classic *Prolegomena*, Ibn Khaldun presents an overview of society in general, the geographical distribution of peoples, nomadic tribes, political ranks, sedentary societies, economic organizations, and what would today be called the sociology of knowledge. He was convinced that the objective study of these areas of human activity would produce an awareness of any patterns repeated over time. With this knowledge, according to Khaldun, it would then become possible to predict the future occurrences within a society. While some of the assertions in his work have proved to be inaccurate, his development of a social theory is, in itself, remarkable.

One of the primary concepts developed by Ibn Khaldun was social solidarity. This feeling of identity with other members of a group or society provides the "glue" that holds the group or society together. To the extent social solidarity exists, conformity to group expectations is strong. Ibn Khaldun believed that this strain toward conformity produced an inner discipline that was much more effective in controlling behavior than any external constraint might be. The individual awareness of the interdependency of all members of a society makes for a strong social bond.

According to Ibn Khaldun, nomadic peoples (tribes) possess a higher degree of social solidarity than do sedentary peoples. This is accounted for, by Khaldun, by the fact that nomadic life is harsh and dangerous. Each individual member of such a group is keenly aware of his or her dependence on other members. The realities of nomadic life produce a person that is willing to sacrifice personal desires and objectives for the good of the group. Sedentary peoples, on the other hand, possess a lesser degree of social solidarity. They are more individualistically oriented. Thus, in a conflict between these two groups, the nomads generally prevail, conquering the sedentary group.

Some of these theoretical principles will appear again in Western writings. Although Ibn Khaldun was almost literally unknown to the Western world until the nineteenth century, the incisive nature of his work was such that other social observers would follow similar paths. In retrospect, a strong case could be made for considering Ibn Khaldun the first social scientist.

The latter part of the seventeenth century and the eighteenth century are replete with important social philosophers. Western man was becoming aware of the possibility of self-study. Questions about the basic nature of human beings, the reasons behind their banding together, and the potential development of human society were being formulated. The answers professed were both exciting and disturbing. Traditional explanations were closely scrutinized; many were rejected. It was a time of intense intellectual excitement. Those of us who live in "modern" times accept the scientific attitude as a matter of fact. But, in the seventeenth century such acceptance was not universal. Bacon, Descartes, Newton, to name but a few, proposed and secured the legitimacy of the scientific attitude. Just as the scientific attitude was applied to physical phenomena, it was increasingly applied to the interactive lives of humans.

## The Social Contract Theories

During this period a number of philosophers attempted to explain the observed organization and development of human society on the basis of a social contract. Generally stated, social contract theory refers to the idea that agreements have been reached among members of a society that they, the members, will adhere to some kind of binding conditions regarding the rights and duties of the governed and the governors, the distribution and use of power, and the limits applied to freedom of action. Social contract theory was an attempt to explain why and how humans become organized into recognizable systems.

The question of why humans organized into recognizable systems elicited varied answers. Thomas Hobbes (1588–1679) answered by claiming that presocial man led a life that was "solitary, poor, nasty, brutish, and short."[2] In this presocial state each individual was in conflict with all other individuals. In order to escape from this dangerous situation, and to alleviate mutual fear and assure their own survival, human beings agreed to unite in a society. Hobbes made no claim that an *explicit* contract was arrived at. Rather, he viewed the agreement as an individual idea that occurred simultaneously in individuals. In one respect, then, psychological factors played the operative role. Hobbes characterized the contract as being irrevocable. This view has been rejected by other social contract theorists.

John Locke (1632–1704) had a less clear perspective concerning the social contract. While Hobbes viewed the presocial human as being, in modern terms, antisocial, Locke envisioned the "state of nature" of presocial humans as being comparable to a *tabula rasa* or, blank tablet. In other words, Locke felt that presocial humans have no inborn propensities for good or evil. He denied that the presocial state was a condition of war of all against all. In Locke's view, humans become what they learn. When humans bond together and form some governing principles (a social contract), the resultant government exists only to promote the general welfare of the governed. The obligation that an individual has, once the government is formed, is either to obey or leave. Under Locke's explication of the social contract theory, the possibility of changing governments exists. Locke clearly distinguished between *society* (created by the social contract) and *government* (to which citizens delegate power and political control). Consequently, government may be dissolved without violating the social contract and destroying society. *Revolution,* then, in Locke's view, was justifiable under certain conditions.

Baruch de Espinoza, also known as Benedict Spinoza (1632–1677), was a social contract theorist who shared Hobbes' view of presocial humans. Spinoza, along with other social contract theorists, firmly believed in the liberty of individuals. The development of the social contract had a utilitarian purpose—to guarantee the natural rights of individuals. Spinoza viewed the social contract as a mechanism for promoting liberty and protecting those natural rights. In the course of the development of his ideas Spinoza angered the leaders of his Jewish community. Because of his insistence upon the natural rights of individuals and his "peculiar" views of God and the soul, he was excommunicated from the Hebrew faith. His unwillingness to recant his views, even in the face of the most severe religious sanction possible, is an indication of the independent nature of his mind.

Jean-Jacque Rousseau (1712–1778) is usually considered the last of the social contract theorists. He too propounded a view of the condition of humans in a state of nature. His view was in direct opposition to that held by Hobbes. In Rousseau's view of the "natural state" of humans, we find a depiction of an idyllic life — one in which conflict is virtually unknown and in which the natural sociability of humans is evident. Civilization, to Rousseau, was the agent of human corruption. Nevertheless, in his *Social Contract* and other later writings, he abandoned this optimistic view of the "state of nature," and adopted Locke's distinction between state and government.

Whether or not the views held by the social contract theorists were valid is, in the minds of some, inconsequential. In fact, there have been several impressive refutations of the entire principle of a social contract. Perhaps the significance of the works of these individuals lies in the fact that they made a conscious effort to explain the genesis of human interactive life. They extended the scientific attitude to a consideration of the questions of how and why humans came to be organized in recognizable units or systems. Once put in motion, this extension of the scientific attitude has continued to the present. In the Western world, revolution, both figurative and literal, resulted. The legitimation of the study of human organization and development encouraged the intellectual consideration of other social phenomena. The social phenomenon of change was one of those areas of intellectual consideration that came under examination.

### The Social Progress Theories

The eighteenth-century social thinkers were persuaded that they lived in the best of all possible worlds, because nature seemed to them beneficent — "Whatever is, is right" — and because men seemed rational. Consequently, they concluded that progress was not only inevitable but also desirable. This view constituted a sharp break with the social thought that had prevailed through most of recorded social history.

The classical writers and ancient Jews believed that perfection was to be found in the past rather than in the future. This belief was based on the doctrine of the fall of man and the dogma of a decline from a golden age. The conception of the cyclical nature of human development was also very popular among ancient Greeks and Romans. The Christians followed this line of thought: Man could never expect absolute happiness here on earth, blessedness is to be attained only in the afterlife.

In spite of these trends of thought, the conviction gradually arose that progress was not only a legitimate goal but also a natural development of humanity here on earth. It gained credence as a result of the growth of rationalism and the development of science.

An optimistic view of human progress based on the advancement of applied science was anticipated by Roger Bacon in the thirteenth century. Francis Bacon (1561–1626) and René Descartes (1596–1650) held that the ancients were no better than the moderns and proposed a scientific and rational approach to the solution of human problems. Montaigne (1533–1592) also centered his thought on the search for happiness and progress in this world and held that this should be the main concern of human learning, rather than the salvation of the soul in eternal life.

Bernard de Fontenelle (1657–1757) and Charles Perrault (1628–1703) stated a more detailed account of the notion of "progress." They concluded that there has been extensive progress since antiquity, and that better things may be looked for in the future.

The Abbe de Saint-Pierre (1658–1753) placed great faith in the *reality* of progress and proposed an academy of political science to guide social development. Following this line of thought, Saint-Simon (1760–1825) held that a basic social science must be provided to guide human progress.

Probably the first descriptive sociological study ever published was Montesquieu's (1689–1755) *Spirit of Laws*. A detailed discussion of the views of Montesquieu will be found in chapter 3.

All these notions finally culminated in the historical philosophy of Auguste Comte (1798–1857). He presented a total view of intellectual progress within his philosophy of history, dividing the past into a large number of periods, each expressing some phase of cultural progress.

What is sociological theory? Where did sociology come from? Who influenced it? How did it develop? In what direction did it grow? What are the main issues that divide contemporary sociology? These and similar questions will be answered in the following chapters, where nineteenth and twentieth century social thinkers are reviewed by contemporary scholars exploring some of the most important questions that sociology faces today.

### Notes

1. Nicholas S. Timasheff and George A. Theodorson, *Sociological Theory, Its Nature and Growth* (New York: Random House, 1976), p.11.

2. Thomas Hobbes, *Philosophical Rudiments Concerning Government and Society*, ed. W. Molesworth, ch. 1, Sect. 11–12; *Leviathan,* ch. XIII. As a matter of fact, there were many previous developments of the *social contract theory* before Hobbes, but he was the first to give that doctrine a comprehensive and classical statement.

# Part I

# THE PRECURSORS OF SOCIOLOGY

*P*art I deals with the Precursors of Sociology. *In chapter 2, J.H. Abraham discusses in a brief synthesis the evolution of European social thinkers of the late seventeenth and eighteenth century, from Hobbes to Montesquieu. The two dominant schools, advocating social contract or social progress theories, were not new. There were many previous developments of these theories before the eighteenth century. However, Hobbes was the first social philosopher who produced a complete and logical statement of the social contract. On the other side, the theory of progress rose gradually as a result of the growth of natural sciences since the thirteenth century.*

*In our opinion, it is safe to say that throughout most of human history stability has been viewed as the ideal and the normal social condition. Change was considered undesirable. Moreover, human progress that actually occurred throughout human existence on earth was thought to be spontaneous, nondeliberate, and without any consciousness of its reality. The idea that the improvement of humanity was possible through the application of scientific knowledge was first suggested by Roger Bacon in the thirteenth century. Although his reasons for suggesting such activity were primarily nonsecular, his advocacy of the application of scientific knowledge to human interactive life presaged a dominant thrust in intellectual history.*

*The inclusion of Rousseau (chapter 3) and Montesquieu (chapter 4) as representatives of the social contract and social progress theories respectively, is justifiable for several reasons. Rousseau was the last important philosopher of the social contract school. It is surprising that Rousseau tried to revitalize that school, after Hume and many others had discredited the contract theories on historical, philosophical, and psychological grounds. It is undoubtedly a reflection of Rousseau's exceptional mind as well as his personal merit. He is the last and probably the most influential and classical philosopher of the social contract school.*

*On the other hand, Montesquieu's* The Spirit of Laws *(1748) is considered the first objective study of human society ever published. He was a pioneer in sociology, anthropogeography, politics, and even economics. He strongly influenced the scientific study of the variations and progress of social life. He also adopted the comparative method, emphasizing the multiplicity of forces responsible for social evolution, which eventually led to human progress. Nevertheless, Montesquieu believed that among all*

11

*these forces, geography, and especially climate, was the main factor accounting for cultural variations.*

*Montesquieu's stress on the relativity of social institutions, laws, forms of government, etc., anticipated the shift from the social progress concept of the nineteenth century sociology to the more scientific concept of social change or variation in contemporary sociology.*

# 2

# The Eighteenth Century Social Philosophers

The seventeenth century can be said to have laid the foundations of the modern western world. The rationalistic attitude of mind, derived from medieval scholasticism, was no longer confined to theological controversies. Free to roam over the whole field of human endeavour, it became the starting point of a revolution in thought. In science there was a more determined effort to devise more simple explanations of phenomena, based on rational observation, experiment and calculation. The unproved assumptions of Aristotle and medieval thought were found wanting and discarded one after another. Nowhere was the revolution in thought more in evidence than in astronomy. The universe of Dante, with the earth as the fixed centre and heaven and hell occupying real and identifiable locations, had to yield to one in which the earth, a comparatively small planet, was divested of the pre-eminent place and accorded a role commensurate with its position and size, no more and no less. For the first time, astronomy allied itself with physics and mathematics to produce a more coherent picture of the universe. New conceptual tools were constantly being devised to facilitate the emergence of a fresh outlook and to account for a different theory of nature.

It might have been thought that, the earth having been displaced from the centre of the universe, man himself would shrink in size and no longer regard himself as possessing a unique status. Quite the reverse. For hundreds of years, man's function in the social system had been predetermined for him, allowing very little scope for individuality. Subject to the whims and ravages of fortune beyond his control, he had to accept his part, great or small, in a system which was greater than the sum of the parts which composed it. Side by side with the Copernican

From J.H. Abraham, *Origins and Growth of Sociology* (Middlesex, Eng.: Penguin Books, 1973), pp. 44–57, by permission of the publisher.

13

revolution in astronomy, there came about a no less far-reaching revolution in the concept of man. Many factors contributed to this revolution: the revival of humanistic studies, greater security of life, travel and the discovery of new lands, in particular the invention of printing and the wider dissemination of culture. All this was reinforced and given greater impetus by the mechanical philosophy according to which matter is composed of discrete units of atoms, all ultimately alike. Having regained his individuality, man was now alone and solitary, master of his own destiny. He was no longer a part of a system; he was the system himself, round which everything revolved. He had displaced the earth as the centre of the universe, and made himself the centre of his own universe. This mechanical concept of man, by analogy with the atom, as the unit of life and existence of supreme importance in his own right, became henceforth for good or ill an essential presupposition of thought.

This breakthrough in the science of matter and in the concept of man — the two were closely related — was not followed immediately by a total repudiation of the older, classical or medieval way of thought. If anything, the revolutionary element in seventeenth-century thought was consistently underestimated even by those who were its instigators, and its identity with the past over-emphasized. Newton's was the outstanding example. As Lord Keynes pointed out, for all the revolution in thought for which he was responsible, Newton always gave the impression that he was looking backwards, not forwards. It should come as no surprise that much of his life was devoted not to science, but to theology and chronology, whose tradition went back to the early chronicles of the Bible.

All the scientists of the day were people of extreme piety whose faith, they were convinced, would be strengthened by the discoveries of science. Indeed, each discovery or advance in science was regarded as a demonstrable proof of the existence of a beneficent Being and as tending to His greater glory. Even Descarte's philosophy with its principle of doubt and the primacy of the human consciousness was inspired by a rationalism that bore close affinities with medieval theology.

In political theory the revolution in thought, though less spectacular, was no less significant. Its authors, Thomas Hobbes (1588–1679) and Spinoza (1632–77), were not, however, conscious of the revolutionary element in their thought. They were both men of conservative temperament, who had a horror of violent change. The doctrine which Hobbes so brilliantly expounded to give a philosophical justification for unquestioned obedience to state and authority was very simple. It consisted in assuming that in a state of nature men are virtually animals, but by virtue of a modicum of intelligence which they possess, they realize that it is better to live at peace than in constant warfare. By giving up their rights in a "free-for-all" state of nature, and submitting to an authority who would maintain law and order in the state, they would be able to live peacefully and securely. A compact or a contract exists now between the ruler and the ruled, which carries with it a condition that the ruler is supreme and sovereign. Whatever issues from his lips is law, for he can't be wrong. His law is therefore a command demanding implicit obedience. None of these basic ideas about the state of nature, contract or law was original; one or other was found in Greek philosophy and could equally have been inspired by the Bible. But in combination and in Hobbes's hands, they were developed into a system of thought concerning society, politics and law unsurpassed for its audacity and depth. As a theory, however, it was frankly materialistic, based on the idea that men, like units of matter, come together and cohere mechanically. Their only purpose is self-preservation, and they are only moved by the prospect of pleasure or the fear of pain. In spite of his atheism, Hobbes was a theologian and a thinker of the old school who did not question, or even feel it necessary to investigate, the institutions of society.

Spinoza's theory differed in important respects from that of Hobbes. Where Hobbes' theory was negative and static, in the sense that it advocated restraint and condemned disobedience, Spinoza's theory was positive and constructive. It specified the conditions of a stable, secure and happy society, based not on fear but on mutual aid and sociability.

Unlike Hobbes, Spinoza put God at the centre of his philosophy, but a God unlike any conceived by man. His conception of God was even relevant to his social and political theory. He did not regard man, in the fashion of the mechanistic philosophy, as a self-contained, autonomous unit, but as one who finds fulfilment only in a community of people animated by a higher purpose. For Spinoza, this higher purpose is the best that our nature requires, and that best is the God in us. All thought, all philosophy, all wisdom had for Spinoza a very practical end, the happiness of the individual. Society was to be ordered in such a way that the conditions of such happiness must be assured, the most important of which are tolerance, freedom of thought and expression. Majority views and opinion must prevail. But whether society is poor or rich, organized one way or another, are insignificant issues compared to the overriding necessity of seeing to it that social life is lived in a climate conducive to the acquisition of wisdom and the attainment of happiness. His theory breathed the spirit of a scientific humanism for which Europe was not yet prepared. It required over a century for discerning minds to realize the dynamic, indeed explosive, character of Spinoza's thought. In the meantime, his political programme was being implemented by the sheer force of circumstance. So his revolution became finally an intellectual and emotional revolution, bringing relief to those who felt constrained by the fetters of custom and tradition. Spinoza did not ask or try to answer the question why things happened in a certain way. He was only concerned to show how things happened, without applauding or regretting the result. Only in this way could we bring a right attitude of mind to them, which must be one of understanding. Like Hobbes, Spinoza's mode of thought and his terminology had an old-fashioned, medieval ring about it.

Towards the end of the seventeenth century and at the beginning of the eighteenth, a subtle change occurred. The scientific revolution had really set in. Its lessons were being absorbed and applied. The accretions and excrescences that accompanied its inception were thrown overboard; only its bare principles were retained. This could be seen not only in speculative thought, but in art and literature. We need only compare Milton and Hobbes on the one hand with Locke and Dryden on the other to realize this. In modes of expression, style and terminology, they are worlds apart. The emphasis in the latter is on simplicity, directness of expression, a plain and unambiguous terminology, not unlike a mathematical equation.

We are not concerned for the moment with literature and art, but with social and political theory. Here Locke's approach was of crucial importance, destined to have a lasting influence. Less original than Hobbes or Spinoza, Locke (1632–1704) had a pragmatical turn of mind which appealed to the rising generation of writers who felt the need to approach the affairs of life in a practical business-like way in tune with the new mercantile spirit of the day. Locke's aim was very modest, to discover what limits should be set to the bounds of knowledge and to avoid speculation that could not be verified by experience. This was the start of empirical philosophy, whose pattern of thought has persisted to the present day. In France, even more than in England, Locke was hailed as the first philosopher who could be understood by the ordinary man and to whose views popular assent could readily be given. It didn't matter if his philosophy was a jumble of half-baked ideas, shot through with paradoxes, which showed how impossible it was to keep to the narrow path of empiricism. But at least Locke blazed the path which could only be ignored at one's peril. It was, however, in his political theory that he came to be widely known and revered, even if it was at bottom a rationalization of a situation that was precipitated by the Whig Revolution of 1688. Locke used the notions of natural rights and contract in a way which made them perfectly consistent with the liberal-bourgeoisie ascendancy in politics. There are natural rights, according to him, to property, equality and freedom. The contract between the ruler and ruled was conceived on the lines of a commercial contract which could be abrogated if one of the parties to it could not or would not adhere to its terms. Locke was the first to formulate the philosophy of representative government. Henceforth all the political movements in England, France, America and elsewhere were influenced, if not directly inspired, by his writings. Like Hobbes, Locke was not concerned to investigate the mechanism of society except in so far as the institutions were defective when judged by the criteria of Whiggism in politics and landlordism in economics.

Now that the political battle was won, at least theoretically, the world was ready for a new perspective in thought, a sociological investigation of history and human affairs. Innumerable factors contributed to bring this about. The conquest of the earth was now being achieved. Vast territories, it is true, were still to be discovered, colonized and exploited, Australasia, Central Africa, the Western States of America. But the consolidation of overseas territories was now firmly established to allow for the further expansion that was to come. The sea lanes round the coasts of Africa, America and Asia were operating regularly to foster trade, commerce and the insatiable curiosity of the European.

For the first time tales, based on first-hand observation, of far-off places and peoples were recounted to the delight, amazement and wonder of European readers. A curious phenomenon was witnessed. The world was being dominated by a few countries of Western Europe. This indisputable, unchallenged and unchallengeable superiority, far from engendering pride and self-esteem, produced the opposite effect. The lives and manners of other people were studied not to prove their inferiority but on the contrary to show how superior they were in many respects to the lives and manners of the Europeans. It was as though the consciousness of genuine superiority bred a no less genuine modesty. As was to be expected, the eighteenth century was also the age of satire, unequalled in the annals of literature. Conscious of the strength of their character and institutions, the Europeans could afford to laugh at themselves by exaggerating the weaknesses to which they, in common with the rest of mankind, were prone.

There was of course a more serious side to this. Nothing impressed the European more than the many-sidedness of human culture and the corollary that the institutions of society, religion, law, politics, manners, and trade were neither sacrosanct nor immutable, that they were human artifacts, and in this sense, artificial. There was a vast untrodden field of comparative study, and European scholars in France, England, Germany and Italy were not slow to cultivate it. All kinds of ideas were appropriated and made to germinate in their minds. Nature, noble savage, civilization, law, religion, politics, customs, were all subjected to investigation, assigned a precise place in the scheme of things and made the basis of a superficial or profound theory.

Nature was the concept that proved most fruitful, becoming the focus of eighteenth-century thought. The writer who made it central to his thought was Rousseau. Neither a historian nor a philosopher, Rousseau gave impetus to movements of thought in literature, philosophy, education and politics which the intrinsic merits of his ideas hardly justified. Unlike Plato, who thought that you could change human nature by changing human institutions, Rousseau thought that, by abolishing human institutions, you could make human nature be what it was meant to be. For him, everything that distorted and inhibited human nature must be wrong. The romantic element in Rousseau's thought must not be regarded as an aberration of mind incapable of facing reality. The idea of the "noble savage" was not entirely a fiction; it did represent a true picture of a condition of life in which the simple, universal virtues could be expressed at their best. The natural man came, therefore, to mean the real man. So the return to nature meant the return to the essential humanity of man, which was to be free from all artificial restraints. Man is born free, that is, man is meant to be free, but lives in chains.

Living in a society, man can enjoy freedom only if he himself has willed the kind of government that will bring out the best in him. This voluntary submission on the part of all members of society will result in a General Will which cannot be or do wrong because it is the collective will of the community and because the participation of all wills in it is a precondition of its existence. Man's true nature consists in the fulfillment of this General Will. A government must be a personal government or it is not a government. It must be formed by all, known to all, and exist for all. The Geneva of Rousseau's day or the city-states of ancient Greece fulfilled all those conditions. He could conceive of no other form of government, because government and society in his view were virtually identical. For sociology, the idea that man lives best and most freely in a community of which he is an integral part, and which he has had a hand in shaping, anticipates the later important distinction made in sociology between society and community. Rousseau's General Will, however, was differently interpreted to mean that man must subordinate his will to the wider whole, namely, the state, of which he is a part — a doctrine which in the hands of the German thinkers became the most mischievous political doctrine of the nineteenth and twentieth centuries. In psychology, likewise, the idea of a "collective consciousness," and equally mischievous doctrine, owed much to Rousseau's General Will.

However, the reversal of the idea of nature, which Rousseau did so much to bring about, was a characteristic feature of eighteenth-century thought. There was not the obvious distinction between the natural state of man and the artificial state. Far from being a state of ferocious competition and lawlessness, the natural state of man was conceived as one where freedom, harmony, and real happiness prevailed. Not independently of this new view of Nature, the idea that there is a law of Nature discoverable by our Reason which should override all man-made law was revived to produce a revolution in historical jurisprudence. The thinkers of the modern era were not in a position, as the Stoics and Roman jurists had been two thousand years before them, to dispense with Divine Law and make use of Natural Law alone to serve as the final arbiter of things. What people like Grotius (1583–1645) and Pufendorf (1632–94) did was more subtle and disingenuous. While not repudiating Divine Law, they merely suggested that the application of Natural Law in human affairs would mark a big step in the progress of man. The separation, however, was complete and irrevocable, not without violent opposition from the conservatives and theologians, who suspected that such a separation would undermine the basis of religious belief and practice. And they were right. For if we were to rely entirely on Reason not only to provide us with insight into how things behave, but to guide us towards the right ordering of life, to invoke any other principle for the task would be superfluous. The Age of Reason had begun.

Two types of causes could now be adduced to account for the course of events in history. The first could be called the Primary Cause, that is,

Divine Providence, Divine intervention and mission in history. The second would comprise the Secondary Causes. Here it was enough to show, for example, that population is related to the fertility of the soil, that a tyranny would manifest such and such symptoms of behaviour and so forth, leaving the primary cause to those to whom it made an appeal. The most ingenious attempt to use both methods, but keeping them entirely separate, was made by Giambattista Vico (1668–1744), perhaps the greatest scholar of the eighteenth century. For Vico it was only possible to treat history through revealed religion if it could be provided that religion was actually revealed to a certain people. The history of the Jews and presumably their successors, the Christians, was a different kind of history from that of the Gentile world. The history of the latter, it is true, is ruled by Divine Providence and shares in the common fate of fallen man. But it is a history that follows a course predetermined by its own inner logic. In this way Vico was able to trace the course of history through all the stages of its development, bringing to his interpretation the resources of a powerful mind, versed in law, psychology, philosophy, religion, and literature. His was the first secular philosophy of history of modern times. His *Scienza Nuova* (New Science) remains a masterpiece of brilliant insight and imaginative understanding. He was able — and in this he was the first of a long line of historians and social thinkers from Hegel through Comte and Marx to Spengler and Toynbee — to discern three stages in human development, which he called "The Age of the Gods," "The Heroic Age" and "The Human Age." For him, human history was a process of cyclical recurrence, 'corsi e ricorsi.' The cycles may differ in detail and in scale, but they all exhibit the same pattern. To take one example: the Heroic Age of antiquity, in which heroic leaders emerged to form a ruling aristocracy, has a parallel in the Middle Ages with their chivalry, codes of honour and poetry. Vico was the pioneer of the concept of social evolution, basic to modern thought. In another respect he was more modern than many modern thinkers. Working within a rigid framework of a theory, he was naturally forced to fit the facts to his theory. But he never allowed the theory to run away with him and in the process distort the facts. He never deviated from the straight path of objective truth as he saw it. For him, as for Spinoza, the primary aim was "to understand human actions, not to weep over them or hate them."

Unfortunately, Vico's work, wide-ranging and profound as it was, received scant attention. It was in France that the transition was effected smoothly and successfully from interpreting history through revealed religion to interpreting it in terms of social origins. The difference between the two methods of approach is strikingly revealed in the contrast between Bossuet and Montesquieu. Bossuet (1627–1704), who has left his mark on French literature through his writings, in particular his funeral orations, was a central figure in the religious and political controversies of the time. As prelate, tutor to the Dauphin, and Bishop of Meaux, he had the power to change the course of European history. The aim of many far-sighted men of those times, lay and clerical, was to close ranks and heal the divisions of the Church. Bossuet refused to be a party to this attempt at reconciliation except on his own, that is Catholic, terms. The opportunity was never to arise again. In keeping with his intransigent, inflexible and uncompromising attitude, his *Discourse sur l'histoire universelle (Discourse on Universal History)* was perhaps the last and greatest attempt to interpret history in terms of the operation of the Primary Cause on human affairs. Bossuet, however, was fighting a rear-guard action. In a matter of a few years the contest was over. The combination of the comparative study of institutions and the tracing of secondary causes, those immediately perceivable and empirically discovered, had produced a revolution in secular thought. Montesquieu was in the forefront of that revolution.

Montesquieu was not a profound or even a consistent thinker. Others in the eighteenth century towered high above him. He had not the literary graces of a Voltaire or a Rousseau, though he had the gift, which only French writers have succeeded in raising to an art, of turning a commonplace into a delightful, witty, and clever saying only through the way in which it is expressed. As a historian he lacked the broad sweep and the massive stamina of a Gibbon, nor did he pioneer a new branch of learning as the Physiocrats and Adam Smith did. But he displayed a quality that nobody in the eighteenth century possessed in equal measure, a powerfully penetrating analytical mind. He took the whole world for his province. If he dealt with ancient history, it was not just with the well-known history of the Jews, Greeks, and Romans, but also with the lesser-known history of the Egyptians and the Persians. If he dealt with modern history, it was not just with the history of Europe, but also with the little-known history of China, Japan, and India. In this way he was able to put his finger invariably and unerringly at the right spot and, without deviating one inch from his prepared position, to show by an examination of human institutions, past and present, how they are affected by laws, morals, religion, geography, and climate. Patchy, disjointed and untidy as *The Spirit of Laws* is, it must take its place beside the great classics of sociological thought, the equally patchy, disjointed and untidy *Politics* of Aristotle and the *Prolegomena* of Ibn Khaldun. It is without question the first work in pure sociology of modern times and its influence and impact can hardly be exaggerated.

I have said that Montesquieu was not a consistent thinker. By this I mean that frequently he was not clear in his mind as to the direction to which his arguments were leading him, and that some of the generalizations he made either did not follow logically from the premises or were not formulated with that certainty that was required if they were to represent undoubted truths. Otherwise the charge that has been levelled against him by some of his critics, namely that he held contradictory views about human nature and societies, can be dismissed as without substance. To take one example: like Ibn Khaldun before him, or, for that matter, some of the earlier Greek thinkers, Montesquieu was impressed by the role that geography or environment played in human affairs. It was only right that he should devote a great deal of space to showing with copious illustrations, the extent of the influence that geography, taken in a very wide sense, has on the human mind and society at large. In this respect, it might be thought, as some of his critics averred, that he was a determinist or, in marxist jargon, a materialist. Yet no one was more insistent than Montesquieu that it was impossible to view man in mechanical terms as merely a creature of circumstance, that climate, locality and other material factors are not the only determining factors in shaping his life. Man's freedom to choose and determine his own fate was for Montesquieu a cardinal presupposition of thought. There is at bottom no contradiction whatsoever between these two views. Man remains free in the very unfreedom to which he is bound. If some of his customs, laws, conventions, modes of thought can be seen to arise from, and can only be explained by, the locality and the material circumstances in which he is placed, that does not in any way derogate from his essential freedom to make these serve his own needs.

Viewing man in society, Montesquieu could not accept Hobbes' account of him as a ferocious creature, nor Rousseau's idealization of him as a kind of angel. "I assume," he says, "that a savage, who has never lived anywhere but in the woods, meets for the first time in his life another man of the same species, and that neither the one nor the other is in a position to flee. Chance, based on the smallest gesture, or demeanour, will determine whether the two men will try to destroy each other or to give each other help. Likewise, the least circumstance will make a people anthropophagous or give it mores." Although in principle man has a choice to live a social or a-social life, in reality he has always preferred to live in co-operation with other people, for this is the indispensable condition of enjoyment, life and development. It is not a matter of instinct. Man's sociableness is what distinguishes him as a man and renders him unique. "The beasts who have all separate interests always harm each other. Men alone, made to live in society, lose nothing of what they share." But to live in society means to have a government.

We have now travelled a long way from Hobbes's theory based on contract, the surrender of rights and absolute obedience. Hobbes and Montesquieu are describing two different worlds, and it is easy to see which is mythical and which is real. Social life must then be conceived as resting on the mutual interests of its members and their adjustments must involve coercive sanctions. Central to Montesquieu's sociology is a theory of social control. For man to move about freely it is necessary to be constrained, "for man is like a spring who works the better, the more it is repressed."

Social control operates through broadly three fundamental institutions, mores, law and religion. Montesquieu was the first to work out the interrelations of these three forms of social control, showing for example that if laws are weakened, religion and mores come to the rescue of society, while on the other hand if religion is weak or less repressive, law is extremely strict. Montesquieu was inclined to give to law a rather more negative role as the repressor of evil, and to religion and mores a more positive role as the promoters of good.

Some of these views may be challenged on the grounds that they are not justified by the facts and they are based on certain a priori assumptions about the function of law, religion and mores. But these are insignificant blemishes compared to the outstanding service Montesquieu rendered in showing that society cannot be understood except in terms of the interrelations of parts. Again, Montesquieu's tripartite division of government into monarchical, republican and despotic is perhaps otiose. But the analysis of the institutions that function within the framework of each of these types retains its validity and transcends the compartmentalization into which he forces his thought.

From hundreds of examples, we will take one to illustrate Montesquieu's supreme talent for social analysis. This is how he accounts for the universal aversion in human society to incest. First he disposes of certain misconceptions. The incest-taboo cannot be said to be based on an instinctive revulsion from intercourse between near blood relatives, nor is such intercourse, as the glib phrase has it, "against nature." The universal prohibition of such sex contacts must be seen to arise from the human situation as such, which doesn't allow for contradictory sentiments to co-exist in the human mind. The relationship between father and daughter is based on authority, which in turn requires that a certain distance should come between the two parties in question. The relationship between husband and wife is based on a kind of equality, which is guaranteed as it were by the intimacy or nearness that the relationship entails. A human relationship cannot therefore be one of distance and nearness at one and the same time. "How should a daughter have married herself to her father? As daughter, she would have owed him unlimited respect; as wife, there would have been equality between them. These two qualities would have been incompatible." The taboo and its condemnation is easily transferred to the brother-sister relationship, though obviously it is somewhat weaker here. The universality of the incest-taboo does admit, however, of exceptions in which the sentiments existing among near blood relatives are such that intercourse between father and daughter, mother and son, and brother and sister can and does occur more frequently than is generally supposed. Nothing that has been written or said about the incest-taboo in the last two hundred years is more than an elaboration, if that, of Montesquieu's analysis. Montesquieu's most distinguished successor in this field, Claude Levi-Strauss, simply takes the incest-taboo as a given, almost inexplicable fact, and attributes to it the primary role in the institution of the human family, and hence of society and culture.

# 3
# Rousseau (1712–1778)

Rousseau was very much of an Enlightenment thinker and shared with his contemporaries several pre-Revolutionary premises and ideals. It would be wrong to interpret Rousseau's concern with the "state of nature" as evidence of a yearning for that lost condition to which men must return in order to regain their freedom and happiness. For Rousseau, man's freedom remained a fundamental ideal but one which was not to be attained by shaking off all society and civilization or by reverting to a so-called natural state. The perfectibility of man, his freedom and his happiness, and the increasing mastery of his own fate, all depended on a clear understanding of the laws of nature. In common with the other *Philosophes*, Rousseau believed that nature and society worked according to such laws; and like Montesquieu, he believed that society could depart from the requirements of its natural laws. Men act of themselves; it is they who must interpret these laws. Because of limited perspectives and insufficient knowledge, they err — i.e., they act contrary to their nature by establishing a social order that violates their basic nature. Rousseau's chief objective, therefore, was to find a social order whose laws were in greatest harmony with the fundamental laws of nature. He sought an alternative to the prevailing order which, to his mind, precluded man's perfectibility and even deformed and violated his nature.

For Rousseau, then, there were two conditions, the natural and the social; and though the chasm between them was already very great, they could in great measure be reconciled. To accomplish this, one must always keep in mind these dual aspects of man. In order to assert that the social order is at variance with man's nature, one must know something about that nature. How can one speak of social man doing violence to

From Irving M. Zeitlin, *Ideology and the Development of Sociological Theory* (Englewood Cliffs, N.J., Prentice-Hall, 1968), pp. 23–32, by permission of the publisher.

natural man unless one really knows something about natural man? And how can one know "natural man" when men nowhere live out of society? It was precisely with the purpose of addressing himself to these questions that Rousseau postulated man in a "state of nature"! This was a hypothetical construct, a heuristic device, by which man would be theoretically divested of his social and cultural aspects. This would yield a concept of natural man which could serve as a kind of yardstick by which to measure the degree of repression imposed by a specific society. Or, what amounts to the same thing, it could serve as a relatively objective, nonideological means by which to measure the degree of perfection and freedom offered by a specific "civil state." If one could determine how men departed from their natural condition and how they imposed upon themselves a social order at variance with that condition, then, perhaps, one could know better how to change that order and replace it with a better one.

## The State of Nature

In the development of this concept, Rousseau is engaged in a very imaginative thinking experiment; but the concept also rests, as will be seen, on an experimental basis. He knew that there was no such state in which men lived before and outside society; in their "pre-social" state men were not men. He says clearly that it is a state "which no longer exists, which perhaps never did exist, and probably never will exist; and of which it is, nevertheless necessary to have true ideas in order to form a proper judgment of our present state."[1] "Natural man" is simply man divested of what he has acquired in society. Think away all his social qualities and the residue is bio-psychological man, or man reduced to what he might have been if he had actually lived in isolation. That this idea is being used in a strictly heuristic sense becomes clear when he insists that his description of natural man should not be taken as historical truth but as a hypothetical condition. Speculation about the primitive state may throw some light on the basic nature of man.

Even savages yield a very inaccurate picture of the state of nature, for despite their primitive condition they are quite remote from that state. Therefore, Rousseau argues, those who have imputed to natural man cruel and warlike tendencies are wrong: they have attributed to natural man characteristics acquired in society. How then does one acquire an adequate conception of the hypothetical state? Fully realizing how complex a problem this was, he asked: *"What experiments would have to be made to discover the natural man? And how are those experiments to be made in a state of society?"*[2]

Such experiments would be extremely difficult if not impossible. Therefore he suggests some alternative techniques with which to approach the problem. One can observe animals in their natural habitat to gain insight into natural behavior uninfluenced by society. Secondly, one can study primitive peoples — savages — keeping in mind that they have acquired considerable socio-cultural baggage. Finally, one could deduce all the factors implied by man's subsequent social development, such as language, and think them away. Rousseau thus sought an objective, nonideological yardstick by which to evaluate society.

If we know something about man's real nature, he reasoned, we can ask whether or not certain historical societies have been suited to this nature. If it is concluded that a particular social order is suited, and we therefore decide to change or replace it, an analysis of natural man must provide the principles by which to guide the process of change. In order that these principles be as free from ideology as possible, we must arrive at this "natural man" by putting aside all those elements which have been implanted in man as a result of his social existence. Otherwise, our judgments would be purely ideological, i.e., we would simply be justifying what we desire and condemning what we do not, and in both cases the judgment would be based on the special position and interests we have in the society. In such a case one would be demonstrating one prejudice by another — an error Rousseau observed in others and wanted to avoid. Hobbes, for example, had, in Rousseau's view, invested his "natural men" with very social qualities indeed.

Rousseau's method therefore required that one subtract all the qualities of socio-cultural origin until only the "natural foundation" remained. In his "state of nature," then, Rousseau was not describing a lost golden age; rather, he was proposing a methodological device by which one might lay bare the components of man's basic psychological makeup. In more recent times, too, similar approaches have been taken: Freud, for example, having employed some premises about man's basic nature, concluded that there is an irremediable antagonism between natural man and civilized man. Marx, on the other hand, as we shall see, also based his theory on a conception of natural man. "Species-being," an idea derived from Feuerbach, resembles in some ways Rousseau's notion that there is a natural man and that the best social system is that which enables him to realize his potentialities to the fullest. Man is perfectible and social systems should be judged by the degree to which they facilitate his perfection. Clearly, if such evaluative judgments are to be made about particular societies most objectively and least ideologically, then some relatively precise conception of natural man is required. This is the task that Rousseau set himself when he advanced his ideal construct, the "state of nature."

How does Rousseau conceive of this ideal state which is to provide insight into man's basic psychological nature? It is a perfect balance between man's needs and the resources at his disposal. He desires and needs only what is to be found in his immediate physical environment. Like other animals, he has only sensations, but no knowledge and no language. Accepting Condillac's theory that general, abstract knowledge is impossible without language, Rousseau postulates that since language is the product of society, one can safely conclude that man in nature has neither language nor knowledge. His needs are extremely simple and purely physical — food, a mate and rest; he cannot conceive of the future and is oriented exclusively to the present. Harmony is achieved between his internal nature and external nature through satisfaction of all his needs; conditions for discord are wholly lacking. Then what, if any, is the relation among humans? Certainly not a state of war. He rejects the Hobbesian notion of the natural state as a "war of each against all." In one part of his *Discourse on the Origin of Inequality*,[3] Rousseau develops his own view in opposition to Hobbes.

In the primitive, natural state men are isolated from, and indifferent to, one another. The incentive to war, arising from unmet needs is lacking. If he has what he needs, why should man attack others? Men have no moral or sentimental bonds, no sense of duty or feeling of sympathy; each man lives for himself and strives for self-preservation. Rousseau agrees with Hobbes that natural man is egoistic, solitary, and perhaps even brutish; but he disagrees that this results in war. Hobbes had not succeeded in divesting natural man of all the elements he acquired in society. War is a social institution and men learn to make war, Rousseau argued, only in society. Robbery, domination, and violence are unknown to natural man; not violent subjection of others, but indifference to them, is the rule. Man is withdrawn and tends to live separately. He is, however, capable of sympathy, which is not rooted in his instincts but rather a product of his imagination. Even without knowledge and without language, man has the ability to place himself in the position of another and to sense his feelings; he can empathize with others and to a certain degree feel their sorrows. Not being a wolf to his fellows, however, does not mean that he is inclined to join with them to form a society. He has neither the means nor the need to do so. In the state of nature, then, men are in many respects like other animals: They are neither good nor evil, neither quarrelsome nor domineering. In this state, there is no education, no progress, and no speech; generations follow one another, but sons are no different from their fathers. In short, men do not live in society and have no culture.

At this state a perfect balance exists between man and his physical environment. But changes occur and the balance is upset. This is not bad in Rousseau's view, for it reveals certain previously hidden potentialities in man. It is not society in general which stands opposed to man's nature but a certain kind of society which divides man against himself.

The harmonious balance would have prevailed if something in the physical environment had not upset it. Man would never have voluntarily surrendered a perpetual springtime on earth, a paradise of plenty and sunshine. Probably, two developments eventually forced men to come together in society: "In proportion as the human race grew more numerous, men's cares increased. . . ." And "barren years, long and sharp winters, scorching summers which parched the fruits of the earth, must have demanded a new industry."[4]

Now men had to unite and coordinate their efforts and they could do so because they had the potential for society. They were intelligent and resourceful enough to respond to the challenge; they discovered that they could not only adapt to the changed conditions but could also, to an increasing degree, bend these conditions to their own collective will. First families formed and then they banded together to form societies; as they learned to act together they learned to speak, and with speech they acquired the ability to accumulate knowledge and pass it on to their children. Man had invented culture. At this stage there was as yet no social inequality. Such inequalities as did exist were within families and not among them; children were dependent for survival upon parents. This was not a harmful dependence because it was natural and temporary. This was the happiest period for man, for though now capable of vanity and envy, he was also capable of love, loyalty, and the desire to please. For these reasons Rousseau prefers this period to the natural state in which lonely and natural man never experienced such feelings; he prefers it also because men have not yet become masters and slaves.

The cultivation of plants, the domestication of animals, and the division of labor generally, opened the way to all kinds of social inequalities which now appeared for the first time. Some men begin to prosper more than others, accumulate wealth, and pass it on to their children. Once inequalities come into being, they create greater opportunities for the rich than the poor; the rich increasingly dominate the poor who become correspondingly resentful and envious. Strata and classes emerge; society is now for the first time divided against itself. Some of the poor acquiesce in their condition of servitude while others prefer to live by plundering the rich. Insecurity and violence—from which everyone stands to lose, but the rich more than the poor—are now felt and feared. Under these circumstances, the rich think of a device from which all can benefit, but the rich more than the poor. Laws are instituted and political society comes into being.

Like Locke, then, Rousseau believed that government originated to protect property—ultimately to protect the rich. Rights, obligations, and rules of property, are therefore products of society, as for the first time man learns to act against another, to attack him. War, therefore, is not a conflict of individual men in a state of nature; it is a social phenomenon. Hobbes is wrong, Rousseau argues, to assume that men made society and submitted to a strong central power to escape the war in nature. On the contrary, man makes war as a member of an organized community—his own community against another. He becomes a warrior only after he has become a citizen.

However, aggression and war also emerge within society and this—what later thinkers called class and civil conflict—is the result of social inequalities. Social relations among men, in which some are rich and some are poor, in which some dominate and some serve, also give rise to hostility and conflicts among them. It is for the purpose of controlling this war that the civil state is established. This is quite the reverse of Hobbes' view, in which war in the natural state led men to establish a civil state for their mutual security and protection. For Rousseau, in contrast, tranquillity and peace reigned in the natural state, where plenty, not scarcity, was the rule and thus allowed for a perfect equilibrium between man and his environment. It was only after this equilibrium was disturbed and finally upset that men created society. The social condition led to inequality, inequality to war, and war to the civil state.

For Rousseau, man is perfectible, and this distinguishes him from other animals. Perfectibility is possible only through society, but man has this potential already in a state of nature. Within society, inequalities come about and the civil state arises. This state is incompatible with natural man because far from allowing for self-fulfillment it repressed and deformed him. Man was prevented from becoming what he "could be" under different *social* conditions.

Rousseau conceives of society at this stage as a new kind of entity. It is a single, definite body distinct from the individuals who compose it; but since only the individual is real and natural, the society is not; it is a product of interaction and interdependence. Since individuals compose it, are its matter and substance so to speak, society can never attain the unity of a natural organism. "It is impossible," says Rousseau, "to prevent each one from having an individual and separate existence and attending to his own needs."5 Whatever unity society has is a function of mutual need, coercion, and — least often — reason. In the society of unequals which has now arisen, this "mutual need" is highly asymmetrical, even spurious. Rousseau writes: "You need me, for I am rich and you are poor. Let us therefore make a contract with one another. I will do you the honor to permit you to serve me under the condition that you give me what little you still have left for the trouble I shall take in commanding you."6

Since such a relationship involves elements of coercion, Rousseau replies to Hobbes that this "contract" is absurd and unreasonable. Instead of inwardly uniting their individual wills, members are compelled to unite in a society which is inherently unstable and devoid of an ethical foundation.

For authority to have moral value the individual will must freely submit to the general will. Social unity must be founded on liberty; and liberty includes the active submission of the individual to the *general* will — not to another individual or group. But this is far from being the case, Rousseau argues, in society as it is today. Men are not united by reason in liberty; they are divided by artificial inequalities and held together by force. Such a society is contrary to man's nature and hence unreasonable. The prevailing social inequalities have no direct relationship to natural differences — differences of age, health, physical strength, and mental abilities. In society some men enjoy privileges to the detriment of others, some are richer, more respected, and more powerful than others; these differences are not natural. Social institutions and conventions invest certain individuals and groups with a "superiority"; these same individuals and groups, in a state of nature, would not be superior and might even have been inferior. In Rousseau's words, "it is plainly contrary to the law of nature, however defined, that children should command old men, fools, wise men, and that the privileged few should gorge themselves with superfluities, while the starving multitude are in want of the bare necessities of life."[7] The unnatural inequalities, perpetuated by the social institution known as inheritance, soon acquire stability and legitimacy. So man, who began independent and free, now becomes the tool and victim of another. "Man is born free; and everywhere he is in chains."[8]

But if society as it is now constituted violates man's nature, will this be true of every society regardless of its form? Is this inherent in all social organization, in civilization in general? Is there some irremediable antagonism between man's nature and life in society, or can they be reconciled? For Rousseau, the suffering caused by civilization seemed far to outweigh its "grandeur." Since, however, man is reasonable, perhaps the present evils could be eliminated thus leading to a new level of perfection superior even to his original state. The prevailing condition was neither inevitable nor necessary. Rousseau proposed, therefore, to emancipate the individual not by releasing him from society altogether, which he recognized as quite impossible, but by releasing him from a particular form of society. The problem was to find a form of society in which every member would be protected by the united power of the entire political organization and in which each individual, though uniting with others, remains free and equal, obeying nobody but himself. In short, "each man, in giving himself to all, gives himself to nobody; and as there is no associate over which he does not acquire the same right as he yields others over himself, he gains an equivalent for everything he loses, and an increase of force for the preservation of what he has."[9] This is the ideal solution Rousseau proposes in his *Social Contract*.

The new society, or social contract, enables the individual to be absorbed into the common, general will without losing his own will, because in giving himself to this common will he gives himself to an impersonal force — almost indeed a natural force. When a man submits to it, no immoral dependency results. He loses little or nothing and gains in return the assurance that he will be protected by the full force of society against the encroachment of individuals and groups. He is now a member of a society of equals and has regained an equality not unlike the one he enjoyed in nature — but in a new form and on a higher level. Freedom and equality are now not only preserved but are more perfect than in the state of nature. There is a vast moral difference, Rousseau believed, between subjection to an individual and subjection to the whole community. The general interest is expressed in the fact that all desire the happiness of each. Yet, when Rousseau set about examining the prerequisites of such a society he made many compromises.

In the new society, Rousseau had argued, sovereignty is inalienable and indivisible. In practice, however, he recognized that it was impossible outside a very small community to have democracy without representatives and without the delegation of powers. He understood that the force of government, though it called itself a public force and though it professed to represent the general will, could usurp power and act against the common good. Government is a constant threat to man's freedom and yet it is indispensable; government is the corrupting element in society and threatens continually to undermine the sovereignty of the people. Thus Rousseau's judgments about realizing his good society were not altogether confident and optimistic. If democracy is open to constant threat from the very government it requires, then "aristocracy" may be the best form of government. This seemed to be the best compromise between democracy and monarchy. Aristocracy was to be a government composed of a minority chosen on the basis of age and experience. But even then, those who govern will have to be guided by divine wisdom and patience.

Even the wisest, most patient, and best of legislators, however, are doomed to failure in the absense of certain preconditions. If legislation is to facilitate the desired profound transformation, then the people for whom it is intended must be neither too young nor too old. In the latter case, they are set in their ways and immune to change; and if they are too young, they are not ready for the efforts and discipline required. Then, too, the nation must not be so large that it will lack homogeneity; for where this is lacking, a general will is impossible. Neither must it be so small that it cannot maintain itself. The critical moment must be seized before it passes. "The whole *Social Contract* favors the establishment of a small society on the model of the ancient city-state or the Geneva Republic."[10] Finally, peace and plenty prevail. Although the role of the legislator is a very important one, his success depends on certain conditions which are at best problematical. Rousseau appears to have believed that the new society will have to wait for some charismatic figure who would emerge in an unpredictable way, quite by accident. If and when this occurred, and if the other objectively necessary conditions were present, success might be possible. On balance, however, he was somewhat pessimistic.

Late in life, when he was asked for some practical advice by the government of Poland and thus had to address himself quite concretely to the question of transforming a society, Rousseau advocated slow change and suggested the institution of several formal democratic mechanisms. Emancipate the serfs, he counsels, only when they prove their fitness for liberty, because men who have been servile cannot become citizens overnight. Do not get rid of the "old" hastily, but change it slowly. The national assembly is to be elected by provincial assemblies; the executive is to be appointed by the legislative; and the king is to have great honor but little power. Finally, those elected are to be closely bound by instructions. In sum, Rousseau sees social change as a deliberate and slow process.[11]

Later, when the French revolutionaries were to turn their attention to Rousseau, they ignored this part of his teachings; and it was only after the Revolution that his emphasis on "organic" change was discovered and elaborated by the Romantic-Conservative Reaction to the Enlightenment and the Revolution.

In conclusion, there are several reasons why Rousseau may be regarded as a forerunner of sociology. As a result of his attention to "natural man" and the methodological device he employed to deduce him, he had an accurate conception of culture — or what man acquires in, through, and from society. Also, he was among the first to address himself in a relatively systematic manner to the origins, forms, and consequences of inequality in society. He saw clearly that the existence of classes and class conflict affected all aspects of men's lives. Inequality had definite inhuman consequences and led to strife and war within and among societies. Finally, he saw the possibilities of change. There should be a way, he believed, to change or remake the society which man's own action has produced but in which he is not his own master.

## Notes

1. Jean Jacques Rousseau, *The Social Contract and Discourses,* trans. with an introduction by G. D. H. Cole (New York: E. P. Dutton and Co., Inc., 1950), p. 191.
2. Ibid., p. 191.
3. Ibid., p. 222ff.

4. Ibid., p. 236.
5. Quoted in Durkheim, *Montesquieu and Rousseau* (Ann Arbor: The University of Michigan Press, 1960), p. 84.
6. From Rousseau's article, "Economie Politique," published in the *Encyclopedie* (Paris, 1755) and quoted in Ernst Cassirer, *The Philosophy of the Enlightenment* (Princeton: Princeton University Press, 1951), p. 260.
7. Rousseau, *Social Contract,* p. 272.
8. Ibid., p. 3.
9. Ibid., p. 14.
10. Durkheim, *Montesquieu and Rousseau,* p. 120.
11. See John Plamenatz, *Man and Society* (London: Longmans, Green and Co., 1963), pp. 387–88.

# 4

# Montesquieu (1689–1755)

With the exception of Giovanni Vico, who exerted no influence on the Enlightenment (and who remained relatively unknown outside Italy until his name was discovered by Jules Michelet in 1824), it was Montesquieu who made the first attempt in modern times at constructing a philosophy of society and history. Vico had read Francis Bacon and simultaneously with the *Philosophes*, and apparently independently of them, had decided it ought to be possible to apply to the study of human society and history the method advocated by Bacon for the study of the natural world. In 1725, Vico wrote and published a work informed by this point of view: *Principles of a New Science Dealing with the Nature of Nations, Through Which Are Shown Also New Principles of the Natural Law of Peoples.* "The nature of things," wrote Vico, "is nothing other than that they come into being at certain times and in certain ways. Wherever the same circumstances are present, the same phenomena arise and no others."[1] Thus Vico perceived order, regularity, and perhaps even causation in the natural world; and this, he believed, was equally true of the social realm: *"the social world is certainly the work of men;* and it follows that one can and should find its principles in the modifications of the human intelligence itself. Governments must be conformable to the nature of the governed; governments are even a result of that nature."[2] Nonetheless, human progress and the perfectibility of man in the secular realm, the central ideas of the Enlightenment, are nowhere expressed in Vico's writings. He remained essentially medieval and theological in his outlook and viewed improvement and salvation as dependent on the grace of God. Though he saw successive phases of development, these were cyclical and repetitive rather than progressive in the Enlightenment sense.

From Irving M. Zeitlin, *Ideology and the Development of Sociological Theory* (Englewood Cliffs, N.J.: Prentice-Hall, 1968), pp. 11–22, by permission of the publisher.

Montesquieu, on the other hand, was a true son of his age, for he had thoroughly emancipated himself from the medieval heritage.[3] His concern with regularities was more in keeping with the modern conception; he sought the *laws* of social and historical development and this was his main purpose in studying the social facts. Facts are studied not for their own sake but for the laws which become manifest through them. In his preface to his *Spirit of the Laws*, Montesquieu wrote: "I began to examine men and I believed that in the infinite variety of their laws and customs they were not guided solely by their whims. I formulated principles, and then I saw individual cases fitting these principles as if of themselves, the history of all nations being only the consequence of these principles and every special law bound to another law, or depending on another more general law." Particular facts become the medium through which he hopes to gain an understanding of general forms and tendencies. In putting forward his conception of these forms, he becomes the first thinker to utilize consistently in his analysis of society and history the construct we today call "ideal-types." His major work, *Spirit of the Laws*, and all his other writings to a somewhat lesser extent, is an analysis based on political and sociological types. This was an indispensable intellectual tool by means of which one could make sense out of an otherwise incomprehensible welter of facts.

There are forms of government called republic, aristocracy, monarchy, and despotism; these are not aggregates of accidentally acquired properties. Rather, they express certain underlying social structures. These structures remain hidden so long as we merely observe political and social phenomena, so long as we merely observe the facts. These seem so complex and varied that they appear to defy understanding. Yet, understanding becomes possible, writes Cassirer describing Montesquieu's conception, "as soon as we learn to go back from appearances to principle, from the diversity of empirical shapes to the forming forces. Now we recognize among many instances of republics the *type* of republic, and among the countless monarchies of history we find the type of the monarchy."[4] What are the principles underlying the types? The republic rests on civic virtue; monarchy depends on honor, and despotism on fear. Again this is proposed in an ideal-typical sense. No actual political form will conform precisely to its ideal qualities; but possibly these qualities enable us to study the actual forms.

Montesquieu views all the institutions making up a society as having an interdependent and correlative relationship to one another and as depending on the form of the whole. Education and justice, forms of marriage and the family, and political institutions have not only a reciprocal influence but depend on the basic form of the state; and the character of the state in turn rests upon these aspects of society. While Montesquieu's ideal-types are static forms employed in the study of social structures, he has no doubt of their usefulness for the study of process. If the study of a society discloses a certain interdependence among its elements, and if a number of societies have so much in common that they may be classed under the same type, then the functioning processes of these societies may also reveal certain similar, characteristic tendencies. These processes and the fate of peoples are not determined by accidents. In his study of Roman civilization, for example, he proposed to show that there are cultural as well as physical causes that bring about the rise, maintenance, and fall of systems of power and even civilizations. Although much has been made of Montesquieu's attention to physical conditions like climate, soil, etc., he sees these as primarily limiting factors and assigns to them much less importance than socio-cultural variables in determining the forms of government, laws, and other institutions.

Montesquieu was perhaps the most objective of all the *Philosophes*. He was so interested in the "facts" that Condorcet once remarked that Montesquieu would have done better if he had not been "more occupied with finding the reasons for that which is than with seeking that which ought to be."[5] Having made a rather careful and empirical study of past and contemporary societies to determine the causes of the variety of institutions, he concluded that there is no single government which is universally suitable. Political institutions must conform to the peculiarities of the society for which they are intended. If he differed from his contemporaries it was in the moderation so evident in his work and in his insistence that one cannot legislate for all men and all places on the assumption of universally applicable laws. He did not hesitate to point out virtues as well as faults in all forms of government. His conspicuous moderation and objectivity provided all parties on the political spectrum with arguments supporting their respective positions.

Though he may have been somewhat less critical than his contemporaries, he nonetheless shared their ideal of human freedom. However, here too he deviates somewhat in his approach. One of his major concerns was power and its relation to freedom. Power should be distributed among the individuals and groups of a society so as to ensure maximal freedom. Men are not free because they have natural rights, or because they revolt if oppression becomes unbearable; they are free to the extent that power is distributed and organized so as to prevent, or at least minimize, its abuse. Liberty is best preserved where interest groups or organized publics check one another as well as the government, and where laws provide for such checks.

Throughout his life, he retained an insatiable curiosity about other countries and cultures; and his comparative approach to society and culture was in a large part based upon his own travels as well as those recounted by others.[6] When he was not actually traveling he fancied himself to be. For example, when he wrote and published his *Persian Letters* in 1721, it was for comparative methodological reasons. Two traveling Persians were writing to their friend at home and giving their impressions of France as a foreign culture. In this way, Montesquieu could at least in his imagination adopt another perspective and view French institutions through foreigners' eyes. This was a way of illustrating the variety and relativity of man's institutions. Though he had never actually traveled outside of Europe, he did visit in 1728-29, Germany, Austria, Italy, Holland, and finally, England where he stayed about two years. His English experience was to influence him profoundly, for he remained throughout his life quite impressed with the English political system, particularly the constitutional separation of powers. When he returned to France, he prepared his chief work, *The Spirit of the Laws*, and then a second one, *Considerations on the Greatness and Decadence of the Romans*, published in 1734. When his *Spirit of the Laws* finally appeared in 1748 it met with immediate and almost universal enthusiasm in European intellectual circles. The new questions he asked and the new assumptions he employed, together with his obvious attempt at maintaining objectivity, earned him a reputation of originality. This latter quality had already become evident in his first work, the *Persian Letters*, where for the first time, perhaps, many institutions of a European society were examined from the standpoint of an outsider.

His book on the Romans was also quite innovative, since he studied Roman society and institutions not merely to describe them but in order to put forward a theory that might account for the rise, development, and decay of Roman civilization. Roman institutions are treated as functionally interdependent and interrelated elements of a complex system. Rome's victories and conquests are explained as the effects of specific social and political conditions. Her success, which required changes in the political structure, led inevitably to decline, and, finally, to collapse. The final collapse is viewed as consequence of the initial success which so transformed the whole structure of society as to destroy the very conditions which made for success.

Montesquieu viewed the social institutions of a society as intimately connected; even forms of thought were considered in their relation to those institutions. Since he was among the first to take this approach, he may be regarded as a founder of the subdiscipline called the sociology of knowledge.[7] He looked at a people not as a multitude of individuals but as a society which could be distinguished from others by its customs and institutions, variables so intricately connected that a significant change in one is bound to affect the others. Political, economic, and other institutions are viewed as aspects of a people's life related to still other aspects. And the focus is most often on the social rather than the nonsocial. Some traditional interpretations notwithstanding, Montesquieu was not a climatic or geographical determinist. Climate and geography, which he did indeed take into account, are treated as extra-social conditions which impose certain limits, at least temporarily, on a given society. The limiting effect of these conditions is regarded as temporary and variable because the further a particular people is from nature, that is, the more developed its institutions and technology, the less is the influence of these nonsocial conditions.

"Spirit" for Montesquieu refers to the distinctive character of a system of laws. The way these are related to one another and to other aspects of a people's life distinguishes one society from another. Although he is interested in the origins of institutions, this is less important than their functions or consequences, as is evident in his thesis about the rise and fall of the Romans.

His sociology of knowledge, however rudimentary, anticipates many, if not all, of the major postulates about a society and its consciousness. There is an intimate relationship between these aspects of a people's life, between thinking and doing. How one views the customs and ideas of a society depends on the social position one occupies and hence on the cultural perspective one adopts. That Montesquieu understands this is clear from the reactions of his Persian travelers. They begin to doubt their own customs and ideology as soon as they leave their own society; and the longer they are in Europe, the less strange do the new customs appear. He posited the social genesis of ideas, and the functional interdependence of social action and ideas; and while, at times, he invokes physical causes, too, these are generally subordinate to sociocultural conditions. He was more aware than most of his contemporaries of the human "cultural variety."

He posited a constant, ubiquitous nature in man which is modified by the specific culture; and within a given society and culture, the position one occupies in the division of labor—occupations and professions—tends to determine one's character as well as one's outlook on life. As will be seen in a later discussion, however, Montesquieu is not always consistent; for he occasionally speaks of laws of nature which he regards as eternal and universal. Men must try to discover these laws and truths and bring their society into harmony with them. This is an ideal which can be approached but never attained. For man, even with the sharpest of reasoning powers, cannot know these truths because of error and ignorance. Man's limited perspectives—the particular position from which he views the world—and his special interests make error and ignorance unavoidable. Much later . . . Mannheim was to suggest some possible ways in which the limited perspectives could be enlarged and transcended; certain groups in society were potentially capable of overcoming, at least partially, the limitations of their standpoint.

Montesquieu, then, may definitely be regarded as a forerunner of sociological theory and method. His consistent concern with laws of development and his utilization of the ideal-type construct were something of an innovation in his time in comparison with the methods of his predecessors and contemporaries. If he is therefore regarded as an important forerunner, this is meant in the sense of his having delineated the subject matter of sociology and of having pioneered in the sketching out of a method. This is the sense in which Emile Durkheim referred to Montesquieu as a *precurseur*.[8] A closer look at Montesquieu's work is necessary in order to see that the attention given him is altogether warranted.

The study of "reality," Montesquieu understood, is an enormously complicated enterprise involving many difficult problems. One of the tasks of science is to describe the realities with which it deals; but if these realities differ among themselves to such a degree that they cannot be classified or subsumed under types, then they truly defy rational comprehension. If there were nothing generally discernible about these realities, they would have to be considered one by one and independently of one another; but since each individual phenomenon involves an infinite number of properties, this would be a hopeless and impossible task. In short, without classification and without typologies, science is impossible and, of course, so is a science of human phenomena.

Was this not understood before Montesquieu? Yes, indeed, but to a very limited extent. Aristotle, for example, did indeed employ the concept of type but confined it to political states. Moreover, even if two societies differed greatly but both were ruled by kings, he was satisfied to classify them as monarchies. His types therefore tell us little about the nature of a specific *society* and its system of government. Aristotle established a tradition in this respect and was followed by a great number of philosophers who adopted his classification and made no attempt to modify it or provide another. As Durkheim had observed, these philosophers "thought it impossible to compare human societies in any respect other than the form of the state. The other factors, morality, religion, economic life, the family, etc., . . . seemed so fortuitous and variable that no one thought of reducing them to types. Yet these factors have a strong bearing upon the nature of societies; they are the actual stuff of life and consequently the subject matter of social science."[9] Precisely because Montesquieu did give attention to the "actual stuff of life," and employ the ideal-type method to comprehend it, his work may be regarded as innovative to a significant and conspicuous degree.

Science, however, requires more than description and classification; it involves interpretation and explanation. These processes presuppose a determinate order in phenomena, such as causal relationships. What is perceived as happening is neither arbitrary nor fortuitous; neither is interpretation the imposition of a wholly subjective order — an order existing only in the mind — upon a reality essentially chaotic and erratic — in short, orderless. This, too, was a basic assumption which guided Montesquieu in his social analysis. In his major work, *Spirit of the Laws*, he not only describes the laws, customs, and other diverse practices of a number of peoples, but attempts also to uncover the origins and causes for being of specific institutions. He does not primarily evaluate but rather tries to understand; thus he suggests the conditions which made possible polygamy, "false religions" and slavery. These may even have been necessary, he believes, under the conditions he observed. Though he tries to be objective, he is also anxious to make recommendations which appear to flow from his analysis. Democracy, he observes, is suited only to small states; therefore, he adds, a democracy should refrain from overextending its frontiers.

Montesquieu's use of the ideal-type differs in still another respect from that of his predecessors. His types make no pretense of transcending time and place. He recognized that the customs, laws, and other institutions of societies vary with other conditions of their existence. He saw certain general types, e.g., monarchy, but saw, too, that specific monarchies vary according to time and place. Therefore, rules could never be valid for all societies or for all peoples. He was as mindful of the constants as of the variables. Regardless of the particular form of a society, the nature of man requires that certain basic needs be met.

As was stated at the outset, Montesquieu's originality with respect to sociology lies basically in two areas: his classification of societies into types, which enabled him to compare them in all their important aspects; and his concern with "laws," that is, the necessary relations arising from the nature of things. Laws do not apply only to nature but also to human societies. In the social realm, laws depend on the form of a society; thus the laws of a republic differ from those of a monarchy. Forms of society in turn depend on certain conditions — a major one being the "volume of society."[10] The republic, as we have seen, has a small population and is confined to relatively narrow limits. The affairs of the community are known to every citizen. Since differentials in wealth are small or nonexistent, conditions are approximately the same for all citizens. Even the leaders of the community have very limited authority and are viewed as first among equals. But if the volume of the society increases — population grows and the geographical limits are widened — all aspects of the society will change accordingly. The individual can no longer perceive the whole society; he tends to see only the interests of his special interest group or class. Increasing stratification gives rise to divergent viewpoints and objectives; and great differentials in private property give rise to great inequality in political power. The leader is now a sovereign who stands far above everyone else. As these changes have occurred, the society has inevitably evolved from a republican to a monarchical form of government. If these developments continue in the same direction, monarchy will yield to despotism which is now necessary to control the masses.

Montesquieu thus sees the structure of and any changes in a society determined by demographic and social variables. The growth in population of a society and the expansion of its geographical limits, a key variable, will force changes in all its other aspects. Although the growing division of labor and the growth of private property (and the resultant greater differentials in wealth) accompany the transition from the republican to the monarchical type of society and seem to be functionally interdependent, the volume of a society appears to Montesquieu as the chief cause of these changes. This is an emphasis which Durkheim later adopts as his own.

Traditional interpretations of Montesquieu's theory have neglected his recognition of the social variables and have drawn attention instead to others: geography, topography, fertility of the soil, climate, proximity to (or remoteness from) the sea, and the like. Montesquieu recognized all these factors as limiting influences upon the structure of a society; they are the differing "constants" that by their presence or absence orient a society in a particular direction. But these factors remained less important in Montesquieu's mind than the social variables.

A "sociological" approach is taken toward all the institutions of a society and is applied to an analysis of custom and law. Custom has certain definite social correlates which are different from those of law. Customs emerge spontaneously from social existence; laws, on the other hand, are established by a lawgiver in a formal and explicit fashion. In the latter case, the "law" emerges spontaneously, too. The more complex social structure seems to require certain definite laws most appropriate to that structure. But these would remain hidden and implicit, Montesquieu believed, if some lawgiver had not discerned them and formulated them explicitly. These laws may nevertheless be at variance with the requirements of a certain society because what the nature of a society requires is a matter of judgment. Men have the ability to deviate from that nature because their judgments are subject to ignorance and error. An element of contingency is thus introduced. A society would be what its nature prescribes were it not for the ignorance and errors of those interpreting what these prescriptions are.

Montesquieu's conception of law as expressing the necessary relation among things retains ambiguous elements. He seems to believe that by studying a society one can discover its laws (what its nature requires) and therefore create legal forms and other institutions which best suit that nature. The creation of these institutions involves interpretation of what a society's true nature is, and therefore is subject to error. In the absence of this element of contingency—ignorance and/or error—man would devise laws in perfect accord with society's nature and, apparently, this would be good. Man's life in society would be wholly determined, and the elements of society would be perfectly articulated and integrated.

The elements of contingency which Montesquieu introduces seem to imply that many can never achieve such perfect articulation. Moreover, these elements lead to no small deviations from the natural laws. For example, though the institution of slavery was present in all the ancient Greek and Italian republics, Montesquieu insists that this institution is repugnant to the nature of republics. If men had not made mistakes in interpreting this nature, slavery would not have emerged. In a republic, slavery is not natural and therefore not necessary. On what does Montesquieu base his judgment? Apparently upon the ideal republic he had in his head. Slavery may be the necessary result of certain social conditions but one of these conditions is the misinterpretation by man of the true nature and requirements of a republic. This true nature, which expresses not what is but what ought to be, has remained hidden from the view of society's members. Montesquieu's social laws, then, sometimes are, and sometimes are not, like other laws of nature, inherent in phenomena. Laws in the social realm are sometimes *above* the phenomena, where they remain unrecognized and therefore inoperative.

The ambiguity in Montesquieu's conception of "laws" seems to flow from his recognition of certain degrees of freedom in man. Men are not mindless creatures adapting themselves passively and automatically to existing conditions. Montesquieu seemed to understand at least intuitively that men also act upon the conditions of their environment and change them. This action involves an interpretation of what those conditions are and therefore, being subject to ignorance and error, men very often bring about conditions which are contrary to their nature. However, the degrees of freedom which enabled men to institute slavery — which is contrary to the true nature of a republic — also enable them, once having recognized their mistake, to eliminate it.

To summarize, Montesquieu appears to have seen two kinds of laws — both "natural" — one of the physical world and the other of human life. The first works itself out automatically, "naturally." The second refers to the "laws of nature of human life" which ought to regulate the affairs of men. But acting in accordance with these laws is virtually impossible due to the unavoidably limited perspectives of men in their respective social positions, and due, also, to the fact that men's acts are not totally determined. Montesquieu postulates a few small degrees of freedom: it is in the nature of men to act of themselves.[11]

Experience and observation are important for Montesquieu; and more than any of his contemporaries he subordinates deduction to these processes. Yet, as outstanding as he was in anticipating the method of social science, he more often than not sets down the facts briefly and summarily without taking pains to verify them even when they are controversial. He was too credulous, for example, of travelers' reports which were extremely unreliable. Moreover, as Durkheim observed, when ". . . he asserts that there is a causal relation between two facts, he does not trouble to show that in all or at least most cases they appear simultaneously, disappear simultaneously, or vary in the same way."[12] Sometimes his types are defined by a single characteristic observed in one society. For instance, being a great admirer of the English constitution, he treats the separation of powers, found in England alone, as essential to a monarchy. English liberty, he believed, was a result of the constitutional separation of executive, legislative, and judicial authority. Apparently he did not see the role of the revolutions of the seventeenth century in establishing the supremacy of Parliament over the executive and the judiciary.

It is, no doubt, always a mistake to trace the birth of certain ideas to a particular thinker. Nevertheless, because he used the concepts of ideal-type and laws with more consistency than any of his antecedents or contemporaries, because he understood the need for comparative studies, and because he advanced the assumption that the elements of a society are functionally interdependent, Montesquieu may be regarded as an important forerunner of sociological thinking.

## Notes

1. Edmund Wilson, *To The Finland Station* (Garden City, N.Y.: Doubleday and Co., 1940), p. 3.
2. Ibid, p. 3.
3. In the present discussion, the author relies, in addition to primary sources, on the works by Cassirer, Plamenatz, Durkheim, and Stark cited below.
4. Ernst Cassirer, *The Philosophy of the Enlightenment* (Princeton: Princeton University Press, 1951), pp. 210–11.
5. Carl Becker, *The Heavenly City of the Eighteenth-Century Philosophers* (New Haven: Yale University Press, 1932), p. 101.
6. For these and other biographical details, see John Plamenatz, *Man and Society* (London: Longmans, Green and Co., Ltd., 1963), pp. 253ff.
7. Werner Stark, *Montesquieu: Pioneer of the Sociology of Knowledge* (London: Routledge and Kegan Paul Ltd., 1960).
8. Emile Durkheim, *Montesquieu and Rousseau* (Ann Arbor: The University of Michigan Press, 1960).

9. Ibid., p. 9.
10. This concept, and others to be discussed later in the chapter on Durkheim, show just how great was his intellectual debt to Montesquieu.
11. See Werner Stark, *Montesquieu: Pioneer*, p. 210.
12. Durkheim, *Montesquieu and Rousseau*, p. 53.

# Part II

# THE FOUNDERS
# OF SOCIOLOGY

*T*he thinkers selected for Part II under the heading of "The Founders of Sociology" represent three different trends present at the point of origin of sociology that influenced its beginnings, as well as its development in modern times. Those three trends are positivism, evolutionism, and Marxism.

Saint-Simon (chapter 5), adopting Saint-Pierre's views, expressed an urgent need for a basic science of society to guide human progress. His description of this basic science has sometimes been interpreted as political science. Although he was not the originator of the many leading ideas later expanded and systematized by Comte, he had anticipated them. Hence his inclusion as one of the founding fathers of sociology.

Comte's (chapter 6) main contribution to sociology was to integrate and systematize the main social ideas held by most intellectuals of his time. Sociology, then, is not the creation of an exceptional individual mind, but the logical result of a long intellectual evolutionary process. However, if sociology could come into existence even without Comte, it is undeniable that Comte is entitled to be called the father of sociology for three main reasons:

1. He gave the name to the new discipline: sociology.
2. He organized the scientific achievements of his time into a systematized whole, showing the unity and ever-increasing complexity of human knowledge.
3. He developed a new approach to the study of social phenomena (the scientific or positive method of inquiry).

The inclusion of Spencer (chapter 7) among the founders of sociology is justified, among other reasons, by the fact that the discipline systematized by Comte was further developed, introduced, and made available to the intellectuals and the general public of the late nineteenth century through the influential writings of this original thinker. However, Spencer built his analysis of society not on the positivistic approach of Comte, but on his own evolutionary theory. That theory is contained in his major works: Social Statics, *1850;* First Principles, *1863;* Study of Sociology, *1873.*

Next among the founders of sociology are Marx (chapter 8) and Engels (chapter 9). As Henri Lefebvre said in The Sociology of Marx *(1969), "Marx is not a sociologist, but there is a sociology in Marx." Marx's sociology is, essentially, the*

51

*sociology of conflict and class struggle. Furthermore, there is no doubt that Marxian thought has strongly affected both classical and contemporary sociology.*

*Finally, Engel's writings are inseparable from Marx. As stated by J. Rex in chapter 9: "Many of the works were written jointly. . . . It might seem that to attempt a separate exposition of the ideas of Engels is a waste of time. . . . Even if Engels were not important in himself, it would be useful to assess his contributions in order to arrive at a clear picture of the original ideas of Marx."*

# 5

# Saint-Simon (1760–1825)

Saint-Simon has been variously and correctly described as "the most eloquent prophet of the rising bourgeoisie in its most generous and idealistic mood," "the prophet of a planned industrial society," the philosopher of the "age of organization," the precursor of totalitarian authoritarianism, and a Utopian socialist.

Engels said of him that he was, "with Hegel, the most encyclopedic mind of his age" and that almost all the ideas of later socialism were "contained in his works in embryo." Francois Perroux, the distinguished French economist and technocrat, has remarked that in the modern age, "we have all become more or less saint-simonians" — observing that Saint-Simon's thought will remain relevant "as long as it is necessary to seek an organization which renews elites, while preventing industry from destroying society and society from destroying industry and either from destroying man," and that with Saint-Simon and his followers "the religious aspiration and industrialism are linked in a harmonious fashion." Emile Durkheim saw Saint-Simon, rather than Comte, as the founder of positivism and sociology: there were few doctrines richer in fertile observations than his and it led simultaneously in three directions — to "the idea of extending to the social sciences the method of the positive sciences out of which sociology has come, and the historical method . . . the idea of a religious regeneration; and finally, the socialist idea."

Claude-Henri, Comte de Saint-Simon, was more than half mad and led a life that was almost as bizarre as the legend cultivated by his disciples after his death. The legend, to which he himself contributed, has it that he was a direct descendant of Charlemagne, who appeared before him, while he was in prison during the French revolutionary

From Steven Lukes, *The Founding Fathers of Social Science,* ed. Timothy Raison, (Middlesex, Eng.: Penguin Books, 1970), pp. 27–34, by permission of the publisher.

Terror, with the words, 'Since the world began no family has had the honour to produce both a hero and philosopher of the front rank. . . . My son, your success as a philosopher will equal mine as a soldier and a statesman.' The legend tells that the mathematician d'Alembert supervised his education, that his valet would wake him every morning with the words, "Get up, Monsieur le Comte, you have great things to do!" and that he proved to Madame de Stael by exclaiming, "Madame, you are the most extraordinary woman in the world, and I am the most extraordinary man. Between us, we would, without doubt, have an even more extraordinary child," adding (according to one version) that they should consummate their union in a balloon.

In fact, the story of his adult life can be divided, in his disciples' words, as follows: "Seven years he consecrated to the acquisition of pecuniary resources and seven years to the acquisition of scientific materials; ten years to the renovation of philosophy and ten years to the renovation of politics." In his last year of life he turned to the founding of a new religion, the "New Christianity," but without genuine religious enthusiasm: it was left to his followers to create from his thought a romantic and mystical cult with its own esoteric jargon and rituals. He always remained a rationalist and a child of the Enlightenment, a philosopher whose aim was the total reconstruction of society and of thought.

Born into an old noble family in 1760 (his great uncle was the famous Duc de Saint-Simon, the chronicler of Louis XIV's court), he fought in the American revolution, whence he wrote to his father that, when his ideas were anchored, he would "achieve a scientific work useful to humanity — which is the principal aim I am setting for my life." On the conclusion of peace, he tried to persuade the viceroy of Mexico to build a canal linking the Atlantic and Pacific Oceans in Nicaragua and then spent some time in Spain, drawing up plans to link Madrid with the sea. With the outbreak of the French revolution, he renounced his noble titles (his relatives fled) and loudly proclaimed revolutionary sentiments. He was none the less imprisoned (by mistake) for nine months.

His chief activity during the revolutionary period was to engage in financial dealings in national lands. He was, indeed, one of the revolution's great speculators, and during the Directory he lived lavishly, with twenty servants and a famous chef. Then, after a major quarrel with his business partner over his extravagance and reckless commercial ventures, he turned to scientific self-education and surrounded himself with scientists and artists. He took a house opposite the Ecole Polytechnique and invited the outstanding physicists and mathematicians to dinner. Then he took a house opposite the Ecole de Medicine, where he studied physiology in similar fashion. Journeys to England and Germany completed his education.

The rest of his life was spent in writing, amid increasing poverty. From 1803 to 1813 he was concerned primarily with the reconstruction of the intellectual realm, as a precondition for reorganizing society. The first need was to develop what he variously called philosophy, religion and 'a general theory of the sciences'—by which he meant a unified system of scientific knowledge, including the sciences of man and society. Saint-Simon believed that institutions are only ideas in action and that "Every social regime is an application of a philosophical system and consequently it is impossible to institute a new regime without having previously established the new philosophical system to which it must correspond." Thus, "the crisis in which the European peoples are involved is due to the incoherence of general ideas; as soon as there is a theory corresponding to the present state of enlightenment, order will be restored, an institution common to the peoples of Europe will be reestablished, and a priesthood adequately educated according to the present state of knowledge will bring peace to Europe by restraining the ambition of peoples and kings."

During these years Saint-Simon's words fell on deaf ears. The scientists treated him as a buffoon and took no notice when he advised them to "choose an idea to which others can be related and from which you would deduce all principles as consequences. Then you will have a philosophy. This philosophy will certainly be based upon the law of Universal Gravity, and all your works will from that moment on assume a systematic character." Neither the scientists nor Napoleon I, to whom Saint-Simon repeatedly addressed himself, showed any interest in the "religion of Newton," or in any of Saint-Simon's successive schemes for instituting an intellectual elite—an elite of "scientists, artists and men of liberal ideas," in conjunction with the propertied, the bankers and industrialists.

In 1805 his money ran out. For a time he was a copyist in a pawnshop and was then taken in to the house of a former servant. For several years, he lived in great poverty and fell dangerously ill, but his fortunes improved with the fall of Napoleon. He acquired a secretary in Augustin Thierry, the future historian, who was succeeded in 1817 by Auguste Comte: these brilliant young men enabled the wild and fertile ideas of Saint-Simon to acquire some coherence. With the restoration of the

French monarchy, he turned his attention to the industrial and commercial bourgeoisie, to whom he henceforth addressed himself in a series of periodicals and pamphlets in the interests of the practical reorganization of society. His attention moved from science to economics and politics.

At first the capitalists and liberals, and especially the financial aristocracy, supported him, for he argued for the primacy of industry and government non-interference. But with the publication of the third volume of the periodical *L'Industrie*, in which the constitutional monarchy and the sanctity of property were mildly criticized, there was a sudden flight of the subscribers and a subsequent trial for subversion, which brought him acquittal and welcome publicity. Saint-Simon and Comte continued to publish further periodicals, exploring in detail the features of the emerging industrial society of the future and exhorting the "industrial class," and in particular the leaders of the bourgeoisie, to bring it into being and demolish the theological-feudal order of the past.

In a sudden crisis of demoralization due to the lack of support for his ideas, Saint-Simon attempted suicide in 1823, but survived for another two years, he turned to the consideration of the role of religion in the industrial society and became much more concerned about the condition of the working class. He also quarrelled with Comte, who derived most of his main ideas from Saint-Simon but henceforth denied this, calling Saint-Simon "a depraved juggler." He died in 1825 and became apotheosized soon thereafter.

It was during the restoration period that Saint-Simon's most important ideas achieved expression. Although, in an important sense, his life's work constitutes a unity, it is his ideas about the significant features of industrial society that constitute his genius and mark him as a founder not only of sociology and socialism, but also of philanthropic capitalism, planning and technocracy. The unity of his thought hinges on his belief, already mentioned, in the causal priority of ideas, both for maintaining social order and for engineering social change. His philosophical-cum-scientific constructions bear all the marks of the autodidact systematizer, and the scientists were, on the whole, justifiably unmoved, although his belief in incorporating the social sciences (what he called "social physiology") in the system of the positive sciences does have considerable historical importance, exercising, through Comte, a profound influence on the future development of sociology. As Durkheim put it, it was with Saint-Simon that "a new conception of (the laws of social life) appeared . . . he was the first to offer the formula for it, to declare that human societies are realities, original . . . and different from those which are to be found elsewhere in nature, but subject to the same determinism."

Saint-Simon's starting point was his perception of the condition of France, indeed Europe, in the aftermath of the French revolution. "The general upheaval experienced by the people of France," he wrote, had led to a situation in which "all the existing relations between the members of a nation became precarious, and anarchy, the greatest of all scourges, raged unchecked, until the misery in which it plunges the nation . . . stimulates a desire for the restoration of order even in the most ignorant of its members." Society was "in a state of extreme moral disorder; egoism is making terrible progress . . ." and the problem was to put an end to the "profound agony which society has had to endure in the period from the decadence of the old political system" to the final constitution of the new.

This diagnosis had much in common with that of the counter-revolutionary thinkers of the time, theocratic and romantic reactionaries of all kinds. But, unlike them, Saint-Simon discerned new forces at work in society and a new principle of social cohesion: since the revolution the "theological and feudal powers . . . have not sufficient force or credit to hold society together. Where shall we find ideas which can provide this necessary and organic social bond? In the idea of industry; only there shall we find our safety and the end of revolution . . . the sole aim of our thoughts and our exertions must be the kind of organization most favourable to industry."

By industry Saint-Simon meant "every kind of useful activity, theoretical as well as manual." Man, he thought, was essentially a productive animal; indeed, properly considered, politics was the science of production. Thus all societies hitherto had been in contradiction with human nature and it was only the society of the future that would render human fulfillment for the first time possible. (On his deathbed, his last words were, "The essence of my life's work is to afford all members of society the greatest possible opportunity for the development of their faculties.") The history of the world (or rather the history of Europe, for, like Hegel, Saint-Simon was ethnocentric) was the history of the development of the preconditions for modern industry, and the motor of change was the conflict between the productive and the unproductive classes.

Organic periods (in which the social and political institutions were "in harmony with the state of civilization") were succeeded by critical periods, which were transitional and marked by conflict and destructive

criticism. The last organic period had been the "feudal-theological system," which reached maturity around the eleventh and twelfth centuries,
but the germ of its destruction was born at the very time of its fullest
flowering: "from the philosophical aspect it is since the Arabs introduced
into Europe the practice of the experimental sciences, and from the
political aspect it is since the emancipation of the towns, that the human
mind has obviously advanced towards a general revolution." The present
transitional period had reached a point of crisis. With the decline of the
medieval system, the leadership had been taken by the lawyers and the
metaphysicians, both equally unproductive and parasitic, who had carried through the French revolution proclaiming the deceptive and irrele-
vant ideas of "liberty" and "the rights of man." The immediate task was to
form a cohesive industrial class, made up of merchants, bankers, engineers, the productive professions and the workers, and put an end to the
rule of the "unproductive" classes.

Saint-Simon illustrated his thesis concerning the functional necessity
to modern society of the *industriels*, or productive classes, and the functional irrelevance of the unproductive, the idlers or drones, in a famous
parable. Imagine, he wrote, that France should suddenly lose three
thousand of her leading scientists, artists, engineers, bankers, business-
men, farmers, professional men and artisans of all kinds. The nation
would become "a lifeless corpse." Suppose, however, that France should
lose instead thirty thousand of her nobility, bureaucrats, ecclesiastics
and rich land owners. There would ensue "no political evil for the state."
Their places could easily be filled, but in any case they only maintained
their positions by propagating superstitious falsehoods hostile to positive
science, and "in every sphere men of greater ability are subject to the
control of men who are incapable."

What was the organization that Saint-Simon considered "most favourable to industry?" It consists, he wrote, in a "government in which
the political power has no more force or activity than is necessary to see
that useful work is not hindered; a government so arranged that the
workers, who together form the real community, can exchange directly
and with complete freedom the products of their labours; a government
under which the community, which alone knows what is good for it, what
it wishes and prefers, will also be the sole judge of the worth and utility of
its labours. Consequently, the producer will depend solely on the con-
sumer for the salary for his work." Thus a wholly new principle of authority and type of social integration, a quite new social structure, based

upon the functional requirements of industrial production, would supersede the old system of hierarchy and subordination. "The government of men would give way to the administration of things," and political action would be "reduced to what is necessary for establishing a hierarchy of functions in the general action of men on nature." The class struggle would come to an end and "the desire to dominate, which is innate in all men, has ceased to be pernicious, or at least we can foresee an epoch, when it will not be harmful any longer, but will become useful."

The influence of Saint-Simon's ideas was immense, though posthumous. There were his immediate disciples, a band of young Jewish intellectuals, mostly from banking families, who had lost their civil rights under the restoration, and who were later, after their religious phase, to become a major force behind French economic expansion during the Second Empire (especially in the development of banks, railways and the Suez Canal). Saint-Simon also had a distinctive influence upon English liberalism (especially through Mill), on Russian liberalism and socialism (especially through Herzen), on Italian nationalism (through Mazzini), on Marx and on Engels, and, of course, on French socialism. As to his influence on European positivism and sociology, it is impossible to separate it from that of Comte, a less original though more systematic thinker.

If his theory of progress was somewhat shallow, if his theory of class is inferior to that of Marx (which some are now inclined to doubt), if his doctrine of the increasing irrelevance of politics and the essentially peaceful and internationalist character of industrial society now has a utopian ring, if the unity of his total system breaks down before the contradiction between the demands of rationalism and the secular religion he thought industrial society required, it none the less remains true that no thinker has had a more pervasive influence on modern European thought and a greater claim to being considered the founder of sociology.

# 6

# Auguste Comte (1798–1857)

The sociology of Auguste Comte has become a classic. Too often, this ascription means that a man's work is revered but not intensively read, if read at all. One recent commentary even dispatches Comte with the curt announcement that if he had not founded sociology, somebody else would have come along about the same time and done so. This comment rests on the fatuous assumption that great systematic thinkers are always lying in wait to take their place in history. Thus, a seminal thinker is belittled as an accident of historical fortune and not seen as a creative formulator of new ideas stimulated by the climate of opinion of his time. At that rate, we could get rid of Moses, Jesus, Aquinas, Spinoza, Adam Smith, Karl Marx, and myriad other figures. In Howard Becker and Harry Elmer Barnes' massive three-volume *Social Thought from Lore to Science*, we find the following ambivalent views of Comte's work. First, they tell us that there was extremely little that was original in the theoretical content of Comte's work and that his main contribution was to give systematic form to a few of the somewhat detached and incoherent doctrines of his time. They accuse him of failing to absorb many of the most important developments of his time and of being behind the scientific achievements of his age in many ways. He was mainly a compendious encyclopedist, Becker and Barnes claim. Then, they turn tail and praise him for foreseeing the following modern trends: the "unity of science" movement; the development of the three "behavioral" sciences — anthropology, social psychology, and sociology; the stress on interdisciplinary research; the forging of deductive models of entire societies for the purpose of deriving heuristic hypotheses testable by computers. And

From George Simpson, *Auguste Comte: Sire of Sociology* (New York: Thomas Y. Crowell Co., 1969), Introduction, pp. 1–23. Reprinted by permission of the author.

to conclude their clumsy somersault, they comment: "It may be said that Comte still haunts us; we are confronted by an old ghost with new sheets."

Comte himself, to be sure, in his later life did much to make some important thinkers of his time consider him a laughingstock. In regard to Comte's first great long work, *Cours de philosophie positive*, originally published in six volumes from 1830 to 1842, John Stuart Mill wrote that if Comte did not give us a full-blown sociology he at the very least made such a science possible by his work. But when, in a later work, *Système de politique positive*, originally published in four volumes from 1851 to 1854, Comte propounded his Religion of Humanity complete with priesthood, rituals, ceremonials, and worship, Mill was led to consider that a great mind had gone somewhat daft. In the 1840s, Mill had openly acknowledged Comte as one of the greatest men of the times. He reversed himself later when Comtean churches of the Religion of Humanity sprang up attracting some serious minds but also many strange characters. The churches have withered away in the twentieth century but their existence darkened Comte's reputation. Yet Comte's feeling for the great need of men for a system of beliefs is no longer considered as foolish as it originally seemed to some of his former admirers, and has something in common with the apparatus that made his religious movement look infantile and, indeed, a little preposterous.

Isidore Auguste Marie Francois Xavier Comte was born at Montpellier, France, in 1798, to a Catholic Royalist family. Hence, his early environment was counter-revolutionary. His life spanned the Napoleonic era, the Royalist Restoration including the bourgeois regime of Louis Philippe, the revolution of 1848, and the earlier years of the Second Empire. He was educated at the Ecole Polytechnique in Paris where like a true young rebel he had trouble with the academic authorities. He was an excellent mathematician — which explains much of why he knew the restrictions on the use of mathematics — but his way in academic life was hard, as was true of other important sociological thinkers such as Karl Marx, Georg Simmel, and Comte's French follower, Emile Durkheim (during the early part of his career). It almost appears that in sociology there is a correlation between having academic difficulties as a young man and the development of important thinking later.

After being early drawn into the salon and circle of the vain, sparkling, and pecuniarily corrupt Claude-Henri de Rouvroy, Comte de Saint-Simon, Auguste Comte soon broke with him. Seemingly endless disputes have gone on and are still going on among antiquarian scholars as to whether or not Comte stole all his leading ideas from Saint-Simon and merely expatiated on and systematized them. A reading of Saint-Simon's work, now made possible in a remarkable English translation by Felix Markham of his leading essays, will show that the shrewd surmises and epigrammatic sayings of Saint-Simon are merely a basis for the large works by Comte. Aquinas took ideas from Aristotle and Marx from Hegel. Each raised these ideas to a pinnacle far above where they were when first formulated.

Comte never held a high formal academic position although he was for a few years, from 1836 to 1846, an examiner at the Ecole Polytechnique. Fired from that position, he lived on contributions from his religious disciples and admirers, including an American named Wallace who bequeathed him a small annuity for his later years. Comte had founded the Positivist Society in 1846. Eleven years later he died relatively unheralded by French academic life. His influence on academic French sociology was felt mainly through Emile Durkheim and today Comte is considered a monumental figure in France. As usual with Frenchmen unjustly neglected during their lifetimes, a street in Paris was ultimately named after him.

Comte's intimate personal life was a disaster and is an intriguing subject for contemporary psychiatry. Twice he attempted suicide, both times in ways that would be detected and from which he would recover. Comte's self-image was, however, strong enough to enable him to continue to work and accomplish great things in spite of (or even, from one psychiatric point of view, because of) his deep psychic handicaps. Like all great humanitarians, at the level of the unconscious he must have hated humanity but sublimated his hatred through work and through seeking to lead men to establish a better society than the one in which he lived by basing it on love and benevolence. Thus, it was not for frivolous psychic reasons that he founded a Religion of Humanity and came to believe that his positivist philosophy and religion would appeal most strongly in the end to proletarians and to women (those who work and those whose work is insufficiently recognized). His deep-seated emotional difficulties and his contradictory internal dynamics do not in the least detract from his sociology and philosophy; indeed, they make his great achievements all the more remarkable. Intuitively, he saw the overwhelming import of emotion and instinct for social life. This view becomes apparent when one examines his contributions to the then-budding science of psychology, where his insights are so acute that he borders on the discovery of the processes of the unconscious though he had no way of learning how it worked, the latter being Freud's contribution.

In an attempt to cover the spectrum of Comte's magistral contributions, I shall stress the following topics: (1) the founding of a truly scientific sociology under the name of positivism; (2) the classification of the sciences and their interdependence of development; (3) the law of the three stages or states; (4) the sociology of science; (5) the sociology of knowledge; (6) sociology as comparative history; (7) social organism, social system, social structure, and social dynamics; (8) psychology and sociology; (9) sociological research methods: observation, experiment, and comparison; (10) the Religion of Humanity.

Comte wrote an abominable French and the English translations tend to read like Comte's French. W. M. Simon in his book on European positivism in the nineteenth century notes that Comte was the only French philosopher who wrote like a German one. Comte never claimed to be a litterateur and I cannot made him into one. By positivism, Comte in no sense meant a way of thinking that assured man complete certainty, but rather a way of connecting phenomena without recourse to supernatural or speculative causes. The chief characteristic of positive philosophy is its search for natural laws relative to the type of phenomena being studied in a science. In the grand historical process by which a subject matter becomes a science, obstacles have been met in every case. In no other case have the obstacles been so difficult to circumvent as in the forging of the new science of sociology or what Comte called "social physics."

Until the scientific method had been refined in the physical and biological sciences it could not be applied to the social sciences, since its worth had not yet been shown. Furthermore, for sociology to develop as a science it was necessary for man to have at his disposal material on a number of different societies so that through comparative observation he might discover what underlies all of them. There was no doubt in Comte's mind that such material had finally become available in his day as a result of the intellectual international upheavals of the French Revolution which made clear the contrast between the new society and the older societies from which it sprang. The intellectual upheaval not only made it possible to begin forging a scientific sociology but made that sociology necessary for directing the course of technological innovation toward man's future welfare.

Comte did not consider that he had discovered positivism as a way of thinking but rather that he was bringing it to its high point by applying it to the realm of social phenomena. Of earlier attempts made in this direction, Comte thought most highly in political theory of Aristotle's *Politics* and of Montesquieu's *Spirit of the Laws*. He also had some kind words for Condorcet and Hobbes, among others. But Comte did not seek anything so chimerical as the discovery of some general law that would subsume all phenomena of all science. The unity of science which he sought was the unity of the positivist method.

The progress of history is the story of the progress of the human mind in using the scientific method in all branches of learning, especially in sociology. Though sociology is the last of the sciences to appear in the great panoply of the development of the human mind, for Comte it turns out that the last shall be preeminent and that the only really universal point of view is the human or what Comte calls the social. Sociology for Comte dealt with the most particular, compound, concrete phenomena — those relative to man and his ability to live together with other men. Although Comte was not one to be preoccupied with definitions, at one point he described his goal as "the rational co-ordination of the fundamental sequence of the various events of human history according to a single design." Another quasi-definition implicit in Comte is that sociology is the science of the human mind whose development depends on human relationships. He also speaks of sociology as the search for the laws of social life.

Only sociology, for Comte, can achieve a generality of world view through which the seemingly heterogeneous physical and biological sciences can be shown to be united in their method. In his own words: "Imperfect as sociology study may yet be, it furnishes us with a principle which justifies and guides its intervention, scientific and logical, in all the essential parts of the speculative system, which can thus alone be brought into unity." Here in embryo is the sociology of science and the sociology of knowledge, for sociology makes possible "the rational cultivation of natural history" by showing how society is the indispensable condition and necessary aim of all the other sciences. The study of social and historical conditions will be seen as the true way to discover how and why developments occur in the other sciences.

Classifications of the sciences had been made before Comte by men of considerable caliber. He was dissatisfied with all of them since they proceeded on the mistaken assumption that each science showed the development of a new or different human faculty, whereas the true problem was their interdependence and their inextricable continuity of development. In addition, lesser minds had established erroneous generalizations about the sciences as a whole through lack of sound knowledge of any of them.

Why was Comte so concerned with the classification of the sciences? For him, a positivistic classification of the sciences would really demonstrate how the human mind works at its rational best, and would regenerate education by showing the necessary interconnection of all the sciences. And most importantly for Comte, such classification would reveal that no social reorganization was possible until the homogeneity (but not uniformity) of scientific method could be shown to underlie all human knowledge.

Men seek to solve only such problems as those in power permit them to solve. The more the data of science deal with the problems of man the greater the resistance of those in power to its prosecution. For science leads to action and action leads to change and change may lead as far as revolution. Moreover, the closer a science comes to studying man the more difficult is rational analysis, observation, experiment, and comparison regarding its data. For, as Comte wrote: "The most general and simple phenomena are the furthest removed from Man's ordinary sphere, and must thereby be studied in a calmer and more rational frame of mind than those in which he is more nearly implicated. . . ."

The sciences have developed chronologically in the following order: mathematics, astronomy, physics, chemistry, physiology, and social physics or sociology. Even the non-social sciences have met opposition during their development from the dominant political powers, and they have sometimes regressed. Subsequently, however, they have taken a new lease on life as power and technology changed hands and their interdependence with other sciences became clearer. The advancement of even the non-social sciences, though historically dependent on previously developed ones, is not assured simply by their prosecution; they must fight seemingly endless battles that grow more bitter as they come to cast illumination on the greatest science of all—sociology. Thus, to give an example from a time after Comte, the opposition to Darwinian biology arose most heatedly not from biologists but from theologians and spiritualist philosophers because the Darwinian conception of man as a primate threatened the bases of their social power. This last consideration leads us to the next topic.

## The Law of the Three Stages or States

The three stages (or states) are the theological, the metaphysical, and the positive. Phenomena are observed and explained in the theological stage as productions of supernatural beings or divinities, and in the metaphysical stage as productions of abstract spiritualist forces (or to use the language of Sigmund Freud, by the omnipotence of thoughts which substitute psychic fantasies for realities). In the final or positive stage (which is not dead-end but dynamic), Comte writes; "The mind has given over the vain search after Absolute notions, the origin and destination of the universe, and the causes of phenomena, and applies itself to the study of their laws. . . . Reasoning and observation are the means of this knowledge." A sophisticated man, looking back over his life history, will see that he was a theologian in his childhood, a metaphysician in his youth and a natural philosopher in his manhood. One may, moreover, be a positivist scientist in a given realm and think metaphysically or theologically in other realms. Nor does an earlier stage disappear from one realm of science because it is challenged by a later stage in another realm, but rather, attempts are made to assimilate positivist knowledge into the theological and metaphysical knowledge left over.

The three stages or states Comte enunciated do not inevitably succeed each other everywhere because there is progress in some areas of science. The law of the three stages outlines the intellectual stations through which the human mind passes on its way to forging a science. One science may be in one stage, another in the second stage, and yet another in the third stage. And internally, each stage has its own dynamism. Stages overlap within each branch of science and among the sciences. Remnants of an earlier stage may persist among certain strata of a population concerning a science even though the positive stage has been achieved there among its most eminent practitioners. Comte wrote:

> During the whole of our survey of the sciences, I have endeavoured to keep in view the great fact that all the three states, theological, metaphysical, and positive, may and do exist at the same time in the same mind in regard to different sciences. . . . In the forgetfulness of it lies the only real objection that can be brought against the grand law of the three states. It must be steadily kept in view that the same mind may be in the positive state with regard to the more complex and special; and in the theological with regard to social science, which is so complex and special as to have hitherto taken no scientific form at all.

Comte here has anticipated the theory of primitive mentality later developed by Levy-Bruhl and then brought forcibly to the forefront of contemporary thought by psychoanalysis.

Comte's attack on the metaphysical mode of thought brought howls of protest and derision from philosophers tied to the past. To be sure, certain theological and metaphysical concepts and modes of thought may be essential for a layman's emotional dilemmas. And thus, Comte's early heavy emphasis upon positivism as the method of certainty for science appears to oversimplify certain aspects of these human dilemmas. But he seems to have recognized this overemphasis in his later work.

As has been already intimated, Comte well understood that the positive stage, in sociology as well as in other sciences, was not stagnant or static. As he wrote in his discussion of the new science of social physics or sociology:

> It would be absurd to pretend to offer this new science at once in a complete state. Others, less new, are in very unequal conditions of forwardness. But the same character of positivity which is impressed on all the others will be shown to belong to this. This once done, the philosophical condition of the modern will be in fact complete, as there will then be no phenomenon which does not naturally enter into some one of the . . . great categories (of sciences). All our fundamental conceptions having become homogeneous, the Positive state will be fully established. It can never again change its character, though it will be forever in course of development by additions of new knowledge. Having acquired the character of universality which has hitherto been the only advantage resting with the two preceding systems (theological and metaphysical), it (the positive system) will supersede them by its natural superiority, and leave to them only an historical existence.

This last over-optimistic assertion shows the strong utopian strain in Comte's thinking, a strain manifested concurrently by the utopian socialism that was beginning to make its appearance in Germany and France. As far as Comte is concerned, however, we may excuse his utopianism on the grounds of his frequent demonstration of realism and scientific encyclopedism. To judge a thinker only by his historically revealed errors is to lose perspective on how much we owe him for his truths.

## The Sociology of Science

When we consider such aspects of what is today called the sociology of science as: (1) the general social conditions necessary to the growth of science; (2) the social role of the scientist; (3) the impediments to the growth of science; (4) the problems which science in general and special sciences in particular set for themselves — when we study these aspects as reflections of the state of society and culture — we cannot fail to see Comte as a preeminent thinker who early understood the significance of social factors to all sciences.

The revolution in science and in scientific method employed in formerly sacred subject matters is for Comte a fruit of the seventeenth century — of Bacon, Descartes, and Galileo. The theological class, which was set apart in the Middle Ages, itself set the stage for the seventeenth-century revolution. He writes: "Whatever might have been the confusion of intellectual labor, and the inanity of the leading investigations of the sacerdotal orders, it is not the less true that the human mind owes to them the first effectual separation between theory and practice, which could take place in no other manner." He follows this statement with:

> Any spiritual expansion supports the existence of a privileged class, enjoying the leisure indispensable to intellectual culture, and at the same time urged, by its social position, to develop to the utmost the kind of speculative activity compatible with the primitive state of humanity; and this description is answered by the sacerdotal institution established by the theological philosophy. . . . We must not forget that but for their activity in the days of its prime, human society would have remained in a condition much like that of a company of superior monkeys. By forming this speculative class, then, the theological philosophy fulfilled the political conditions of a further progression of the human mind.

The theological stage, however, proves its own undoing by failing to be able to settle the problems which arise in and through it and by the metaphysical problems which arise from it which cannot be answered by the existent theology. Though the metaphysical philosophy has its own dangers, intellectual and moral, it in turn raises questions which cannot be answered within the metaphysical orbit but only by beginning the systematic observation, comparison, and experimentation which led into the stage of positivism. The theological stage when paramount is always contingent upon the supremacy of military regimes. The gods and the generals go hand in hand. The metaphysical stage is marked by religious and political upheaval whereas the positive stage is marked by the beginning of the supremacy of industry and technology.

Thus, Comte had already seen what latter-day historians began to see in recent decades: there was no "Dark Age" in western civilization, since opposition to theology and metaphysics was always being carried on somewhere, somehow, by the intellectual curiosity of the human mind for proof and evidence of the laws governing the universe and human life. One could even make a case for Comte's having seen the significance of the rise of what he calls "heretical Protestantism" for the growth of the positive spirit and of modern commerce and industry. The theory of the significance of the Protestant ethic for the rise of capitalism is not the discovery of Max Weber, as has been claimed.

Unlike Marx, Comte placed his faith in progress through the orderly permeation of the positive philosophy among common men and women rather than through a proletarian revolution. "Order and Progress" are Comte's mottoes, as opposed to "class struggle" and "the proletarian revolution." Yet, this stand which stresses "order" did not endear him to conservatives or reactionaries.

Comte's entire discussion of the effect of what he called "The Industrial Movement" on human personality, domestic life and the family; the abolition of the caste system; internationalism; industrial policy; Catholicism; administration; the growth of banking and public credit; the upsurge of invention (firearms, printing, maritime discovery); colonialism; slavery; and the flowering of the arts still deserves close reading despite the meandering, prolix style laden with repetition, and the uninviting character of his language.

### The Sociology of Knowledge

In his essay summarizing the range of the sociology of knowledge in the book entitled *Modern Sociological Theory*, Professor Franz Adler finds the major roots of this field in the Durkheim school of sociology, in Marx and the Marxists, in the anti-Marxists, especially Max Scheler and Paul Honigsheim, and in Karl Mannheim. Comte is given less than scant treatment and is even treated as the parent of contemporary neo-positivism for which actually, as already noted, he had absolutely no responsibility at all except that the neo-positivists took over his title for their philosophy. When Comte talks about positivism, it cannot too often be stressed that he means an attitude of mind towards science and the explanation of nature, man, and society, and not some predilection for mathematical precision, especially not in sociology. In fact, Comte expressly makes a distinction between the search for certainty in science and the mistaken search for numerical precision.

Even the excellent book on the sociology of knowledge by Berger and Luckman, *The Social Construction of Reality*, makes no mention at all of Comte. Yet, from the standpoint of both the particular sciences and their ideologies, and the standpoint of ideology in general, Comte is the originator of the sociology of knowledge. The three leading general ideologies are for Comte, as one might expect, the theological, the metaphysical, and the positive. Comte realizes, like Marx and Engels, that "Social being determines social consciousness" not unilaterally but rather interdependently. Indeed, the whole aim of his positive philosophy is to help men develop a society in which "positivistic consciousness" determines social being — a society where if the scientist, especially the social scientist, is not king, at least every common man is to some degree a practitioner or respects the findings of social science. Even in a particular science where enough intellectual and methodological momentum has been gained inside the science itself to promulgate new problems and expand knowledge, it remains true that the science in its existent organizational state is interwoven with some general state of the society's fundamental beliefs and sentiments.

Max Scheler's distinctions between social conditions or what he calls "real factors" which do not determine knowledge but merely make it possible, and "ideal factors" where the succession of thought by new thought determines the state of knowledge, do not go as far as Comte's position. For Comte, social conditions determine whether a science can develop, to what degree it can develop, and the uses to which it can be put. Though the validity of propositions in knowledge may not be specifically determined by social conditions, the addiction to validity is itself determined by them. Once under way, the progress of positivist knowledge cannot be permanently stopped or pushed back, but neither can it continue to advance without social conditions adequate to the intellectual needs of its adherents.

As for ideologies in general, men of primitive power pursue theological thinking because they need to retain their dominance in social life and to keep other men in subjection. Only long struggles for positivistic ideology by men of foresight serve to achieve social conditions under which metaphysical propositions give way to positivistic ones. Conversely, the positivistic stage is reached in any science — and especially in sociology — through a continual reorganization of society made possible by the pursuit of sociology and its application to practical problems, particularly problems in the organization of knowledge, its propagation, and its being passed on from generation to generation. Thus, Jean Lacroix is correct in his little book, *La Sociologie d'Auguste Comte*, published in Paris in 1956, when he writes that in final analysis positivism is essentially a pedagogy.

Neither here under the heading of the sociology of knowledge nor in other parts of sociology is it my intent to start a "back to Comte" movement in sociology like the ill-fated "back to Kant" movement in philosophy but rather to suggest the feasibility of a "forward with Comte" movement by pushing ahead with the implications of his thought. But to push ahead, his thoughts must be known and must once again become coins of the sociological realm.

## Sociology as Comparative History

Comte is often treated as if his chief contribution were to the philosophy of history, and he has indeed been called the French Hegel. But Comte was interested in the study of history primarily as a basis for discovering the laws governing the social organism, social structure, and social dynamics. History is a laboratory for the sociologist in that it enables him to compare different types of society, to discover their common elements, and to account for the differences in their structure and in their dynamic flow.

Why did the old patterns of western society break down and wither away and give rise to modern industrial society? This question is basic to Comte's development of sociology, and in answering it, he refuses to become bogged down in historical minutiae. What Comte is looking for are the laws of social existence, and he writes:

> We must avoid confounding the abstract research into the laws of social existence with the concrete histories of human societies, the explanation of which can result only from a very advanced knowledge of the whole of these laws. Our employment of history in this inquiry, then, must be essentially abstract. But the laws of social existence cannot be discovered until the entire system of the preceding sciences has been formed, and the whole mass of historical information offered as material for its analysis. The function of Sociology is to derive from this mass of unconnected material, information which, by the principles of the biological theory of man, may yield the laws of social life.

The scientific comparison of immutable landmarks throughout the whole of past human experience will afford a direction and a rallying point for sociology, and will reveal the fundamental structure of all societies, the reasons for the peculiarities of each, and the goals for social reorganization which modern sociology can posit for man. Modern institutions are not all suitable to man's needs and their adaptation can be achieved only by understanding the irrelevancy of certain theologically and metaphysically based institutions to the positive spirit of modern industrialism. Here is contained a first intimation of the concept of anomy that Durkheim enunciated at the end of his work in 1893 on the division of labor in society, a concept which Durkheim himself indicated was not his own discovery but rather an expatiation on Comte's theme.

For almost a century Comte has been the butt of bad jokes by sorry historical academicians. Thus, there is more than poetic justice, there is scientific justice, in the recent discovery of the importance of sociological considerations to the understanding of history as a subject. We now attempt to bring to life even the most minute of historical events by showing them in the context of the type of society in which they occur and their concurrence or discordance with other elements of existing institutions and orders of social relationships. Thus, the French Revolution, which brought down the old order and ushered in the new, was not simply a political or economic phenomenon but the result of massive disjunctions among the various segments of the old society. Were Comte alive today he might point to the Russian and Chinese Revolutions as proof of what happens when a weary ideological order impedes the forces of material and intellectual progress which are impinging upon it. Comte had an intellectual quality sadly lacking among too many contemporary American sociologists: learned vision.

For the fact-burdened peddler of history, the historicist, history consists of unique events, but for Comte, it consists of a laboratory for research into the general trends and tendencies of whole societies. In fact, one might go so far as to say that, for Comte, unique events when thoroughly investigated are not unique at all. Comte's sociology is societal, not a series of isolated monographs on specific subjects or compartments studied in isolation. It is the search for human perfectibility and not a disembodied discipline far above the madding crowd and impervious to the vital impact of new technology, new administrative techniques, the rise of social classes, and the struggle for power among discordant factions. A new elite of men of learning, each pursuing his appointed task, yet under the aegis of sociology as a manifestation of their mutual interdependence, would also be pursuing the general positive philosophy and make possible human progress never before contemplated.

It is easy to accuse Comte of grand historical generalizations by failing to realize that we all have to live by some such generalizations. He had the unmitigated courage to spell out the details of these generalizations and what they boded for the future. He also saw the necessity that such generalizations be openly arrived at. Open generalizations openly arrived at — not secret, undigested generalizations covertly guiding specific little pieces of research — were the aim and goal of the new science which he named and sociologists today pursue, though generally not in the manner he intended. Comte was not a mediocre theorist but a genius who took in the large overall view, and like all geniuses he often, to be sure, overstepped the boundaries of his otherwise good sense.

## Social Organism, Social System, Social Structure, and Social Dynamics

Long before late nineteenth-century sociologists began to discuss the concept of society as an organism and years before Darwin propounded his theories, Auguste Comte hit upon the idea of conceiving society as an organism. Thus, the idea of a "social system" which gave such notoriety to the American Talcott Parsons and his cohort of terminological enthusiasts, is already presaged in Comte. He uses the term "social organism" to describe society as a consensus of parts, an interconnection of institutions similar to the interconnection of functions in an organism. He does not reach the absurd lengths of certain later nineteenth-century and even early twentieth-century sociologists who by argument from analogy found all parts of living organisms existing in society, to the point where Brunschwig found the church to represent the female sex and the state the male sex. Comte feels no science could ever be explained wholly through argument by analogy. He understands that each science has its own subject matter which inevitably leads to investigation of new phenomena by newly appropriate methods, and he holds to the self-subsistent character of every science internally even though externally its further development depends upon the state of society and the supremacy of the positivist doctrine in philosophy. He uses the term "social system" to describe the subject of social statics which, he writes, "consists in the investigation of the laws of social action and reaction of the different parts of the social system." Comte writes further that, "The scientific principle of the relations between the political and the social condition is simply this — that there must always be a spontaneous harmony between the whole and the parts of the social system, the elements of which must inevitably be, sooner or later, combined in a mode entirely conformable to their nature." This mutual interaction, however, is not always harmonious. Lack of harmony in the functioning of parts will result in change or even upheaval. This idea leads to Comte's discussion of the two main fields of sociology — social statics and social dynamics.

Social statics is concerned with the study of social organization. But social organization must be looked at as a totality. Comte writes:

> There can be no scientific study of society, either in its conditions or its movements, if it is separated into portions, and its divisions are studied apart. . . . Materials may be furnished by the observation of different departments; and such observation may be necessary for that object, but it cannot be called science. The methodical division which takes place in the simple inorganic sciences is thoroughly irrational in the recent and complex science of society and can produce no results. The day may come when some sort of subdivision may be practicable and desirable; but it is impossible for us now to anticipate what the principle of distribution may be; for the principle itself must arise from the development of the science; and that development can take place not otherwise than by the formation of the science as a whole. The complete body will indicate for itself, at the right season, the particular points which need investigation and then will be the time for such special study as may be required . . . It is no easy matter to study special phenomena in the only right way — viewing each element in the light of the whole system. It is no easy matter to exercise such vigilance so that no one of the number of contemporary aspects shall be lost sight of. But it is the right and the only way; and we may perceive in it a clear suggestion that this lofty study should be reserved for the highest order of scientific minds, better prepared than others, by wise educational discipline, for sustained speculative efforts, aided by an habitual subordination of the passions to the reason.

Sociology, for Comte, is a dynamic study in two senses; it will change the conditions of man in society through social reorganization and it is itself the study of how social changes necessarily take place as interrelated structures and functions break down and require rearrangement. Social dynamics cannot be adequately understood without knowledge of what he calls the spontaneous order of human society or social statics. The basic social elements whose study make up social statics are: (1) the instinctual and emotional make-up of man's biological and psychological existence; (2) religion as regulative; (3) property and material life; (4) the family as the basic unit of social organization based upon the sexual and parental relationships; (5) language whose origin is familial and whose

development is social in the broader sense; (6) large-scale social organizations or secondary groups, which are economic (through the distribution of employments) and governmental; (7) social existence seen as a
whole; (8) the limits of variation within social statics.

All these elements are subject to the dynamic workings of society
through change and progress. And although they make society possible,
analyses of these static elements do not give us the clue to the true heart of
the natural progress of human society. The causes for the dynamism
inherent in man's social situation involve climate, physical environment,
population growth through an increased birth rate and a decreased mor-
tality rate, technology, the steady advancement of science from the theological to the positivist stage, and the growth of law and civilian government. Thus, Comte is led into detailed analyses of the whole pageant of
western history, arriving finally at the notion that our "present confusion" can be resolved only by a new morality based upon the benevolent
political philosophy of positivism which will give wise systematic direction to the next great movement in human progress.

### Psychology and Sociology

The famous early American sociologist Lester F. Ward, who was
known for his strict scientific scruples and who rarely indulged himself by
failing to understand the work of other thinkers, nevertheless made an
egregious error by holding Comte's sociology to be grounded in an inade-
quacy of psychology. Ward was far off the mark here. The difficulty
probably arose because Comte, as far as possible, avoided use of the term
"psychology." The unhappy term he uses is "cerebral biology" and he
severely criticizes most of what was called psychology in his time as
incapable of being a science. He sees the importance of studying the
relations of the affectual states of man to his intellectual faculties but does
not consider that to be psychology, although, as we shall see, his discussion throughout on this relationship is psychologically accurate to the
point of being a forerunner of certain contemporary thinking. Comte
propounds some very general ideas on psychology or cerebral biology as
a science which have striking analogues in psychoanalysis, the psychology that has revolutionized man's concept of himself. His early British
follower, G. H. Lewes, wrote in 1853: "Positive philosophy . . . if not in
a condition, as yet, to elaborate a science of psychology . . . clears the
way for one, by pointing out the direction which investigation must
take." That direction was not forthrightly taken until a half-century later

when Freud came to put flesh on the bare bones of Comte's affectual psychology.

The Enlightenment enthroned Reason—a well-nigh disembodied Reason—as the criterion of judgement concerning the worth of a human society. Comte certainly was not a child of this Enlightenment. He begins his own psychological discussion with a searching criticism of Descartes for falling into the trap of the rationalistic fallacy. Comte deeply appreciated the "glorious service" rendered by Descartes in mathematics and physics. But in psychological matters Descartes retreated, in Comte's view, to theological and metaphysical stages by representing man as a reasoning animal. For all his immense belief in man's being capable of modification and improvement in his social relations through intellect and reason (that is, through being guided by positivistic thinking), Comte saw, nevertheless, that it is the human instincts which are paramount originally and which remain basic to the flowering of intellect and reason themselves. Here is a foreshadowing of Freud's view that the unconscious and the instincts are the foundation of all human mental energy with their most ennobling derivatives being science, art, and abstract thought. Says Comte:

> The affections, the propensities, the passions, are the great springs of human life. . . . Their spontaneous and independent impulse is indispensable to the first awakening and continuous development of the various intellectual faculties, by assigning to them a permanent end, without which—to say nothing of their general direction—they would remain dormant in the majority of men. It is even but too certain that the least noble and most animal propensities are habitually the most energetic, and therefore the most influential.

The separation of instinct from reason is for Comte a throwback to the metaphysical mode of thinking. Human nature is induced in various directions by distinct and independent powers, among which equilibrium is established with extreme difficulty. Here again is a striking similarity to Freud's view of the interplay of id, ego, and superego. Yet Freud knew almost nothing about Comte's systematic work. Even Comte's insight in his work on positive polity, that dreams show the preponderance of the affective faculties over the intellectual faculties, is not mentioned in Freud's presumably exhaustive history in the first chapter of *The Interpretation of Dreams*.

Comte followed hard upon the heels of the psychological theories of

Franz Joseph Gall, the founder of phrenology, which was then a respectable subject seeking to topographically chart out areas of the brain in order to establish where specific human faculties and character traits had their seat. Phrenological topography never worked out and this false trial led Comte somewhat astray.

The new science of sociology, wrote Comte, is rooted in biology. Everybody, he notes, seems willing to agree to this statement and then goes about neglecting it in practice. Comte thinks this neglect arises from the most conspicuous defect of biological science — failure to deal adequately with intellectual and moral phenomena — and goes about seeking to rectify it. When finally this imperfection is removed, cerebral biology or psychology will be able to provide the starting point of all social speculation, in accordance with the analysis of the social faculties of man and of the organic conditions which determine their character. But sociology is more than psychology for Comte. From psychology, sociology learns to understand the agents of collective phenomena and then shows how the social environment affects the workings of the instincts and determines the course of human progress in history.

In *Positive Polity*, Comte amplified his ideas on psychology, stressing once again the predominance of the emotive over the merely intellectual functions. Here he divides emotional life into the personal and the social; the personal side Comte calls "egoism," the social side, "altruism." This second term was later taken over by Herbert Spencer, who, in a most unusual act, acknowledged his debt to Comte. Egoism and altruism, for Comte, are in permanent conflict — an idea which contains another basic tenet of psychoanalysis, the clash of narcissism with social demands on the individual.

For Comte there are three sets of instincts: personal, intermediate, and social. The personal are the instinct of self-preservation, the sexual instinct, the maternal instinct, the aggressive instinct, and the industrial instinct. The last sounds peculiarly like the instinct of workmanship proclaimed by Thorstein Veblen seventy-five years later in his book by that name. The intermediate instincts are pride (love of power) and vanity (love of approbation). The social instincts are attachment to other human beings, veneration or voluntary submission, and benevolence.

The types of individual character which emerge in social life are principally determined by the constitution of the emotional area of human life. The latter's development, in turn, depends upon the influences exerted by the intellectual and moral faculties which are themselves reflections of the social statics and dynamics pervasive in a given society. Yet, human will, no matter how it is socialized, is the acting out of desire after mental deliberation has decided on the propriety of some predominant impulse — a prevision of the psychoanalytic doctrine of rationalization. Though intellectual functions inspire special desires, they are deficient in the energy necessary to induce action which depends solely on the emotional impulse.

## Sociological Research Methods: Observation, Experiment, and Comparison

Discussion of the scientific methodology proposed by Comte for sociology will place it within the general perspective of his total doctrine, show that the view that Comtean sociology is antagonistic to contemporary research methods in sociology is mistaken, and reveal how really "modern" and even "contemporary" his methodology was. In short, Comte is not a part of a bygone intellectual tradition which gives sociologists a past to wallow in; he is part and parcel of valuable intellectual baggage they carry around today.

According to Comte, two main methods are available to social physics or sociology: direct methods which are peculiar to the subject itself and indirect methods which draw materials from other sciences and incorporate them into the subject's direct methods. The direct methods are: (1) observation, (2) experiment, (3) comparison.

In the use of observation, the first problem is to develop ways and means of assuring that different sociologists will be able to see, hear, and experience the same phenomena. Observation of such a uniform kind cannot be assured unless it takes place on the basis of established sociological laws, no matter how elementary they are at the beginning. Without laws and the testing of hypotheses based upon them, we would amass a scattering of random observations. Comte writes: "Social science requires, more than any other, the subordination of observation to the statical and dynamical laws of phenomena. No social fact can have any scientific meaning till it is connected with some other social fact; without such connection it remains a mere anecdote, involving no rational utility." Attention must be called here to the fact that Durkheim lifted this last idea bodily from Comte in his own *Rules of Sociological Method* a half-century later and that with majestic invalidity Durkheim has since been credited with being its author.

At first, Comte continues, good observers will be rare because they cannot systematize their observations through laws and hypotheses but this situation will improve as the science develops. This shortcoming has its good side since it will keep petty minds from meddling with this most difficult subject. A mind suitably trained in scientific method becomes able to convert almost all impressions from the events of life into sociological data when experience is combined with an innate talent to interrelate them.

When Comte comes to the discussion of experimentation in sociological research, he distinguishes with unerring vision the use of both "natural experiments," as John Stuart Mill called happenings in history, over which the sociologist has no control but which he uses as data and "artificial experiments" or what are today thought of as "controlled experiments."

Employing indirect methods of experimentation in observation of diseased states of the social organism, Comte demonstrates a keen appreciation of the use of the so-called abnormal for the discovery of the normal—a project which Durkheim has for long been credited with systematically initiating and which Freud used to such magnificent advantage in arriving at an approximation of a normal ego. Comte's discussion of this topic contains the kernel of one aspect of the idea of anomy and also supports Freud's belief that a singular case could often be found to be typical of a whole range of cases and make continuous replication unnecessary.

In his discussion of the use of comparison as part of scientific method in sociology, Comte begins by pointing out the great value of comparing whatever rudiments of social life we find among the lower animals with that found among humans — a method which later was for a time much in vogue and was used in studies made of the social life of ants, bees, and the lower primates. Comte thought the first germs of social relations could be discovered among the lower animals, and this method has since proven of some advantage in such subsidiary fields of sociological study as the family, the division of labor, and the socialization process. In a revolutionary statement, he points out that the discovery of man's relation to the lower animals will do much to undermine what he calls the "insolent pride" of the ruling classes who consider themselves a special species above mankind. With modesty, he concludes that since he can as yet offer only the first conception of a science of sociology, he can himself make little use of this kind of comparison, but this inability on his part only underlines the necessity to point it out lest its omission should hamper the advancement of the subject he was founding. Comte was already stressing man's similarities to the lower animals years before Darwin spelled out his laws of biological evolution.

The chief use Comte sees of the method of comparison is the discovery — through the study of coexisting states of society in different parts of the world — of social structures, social classes, social functions, and those patterns of social behavior which are universal. "The human mind," he writes, "is uniform in the midst of all diversities of climate, and even of race, such diversities having no effect upon anything more than the rate of progress." Still comparison of coexisting societies will not give us the chief scientific tool of positive sociology: the comparison of consecutive stages through which society passes. Here the historical method of comparison is paramount. Our existing state cannot be understood simply through study of it as it is, but only by seeing it as part of the series of social states from which it has emerged and which have left their imprint upon our minds. Every law of social succession disclosed by the historical method must be unquestionably connected, directly or indirectly, with the positivist theory of human nature already discussed here under the heading of Comte's view of psychology. Thus, the main strength of sociological demonstrations must ever lie in the concordance of the conclusions of historical analysis with the preparatory conceptions of the psychological theory. This part of the method of comparison, the historical method, will enable us to analyze the most complex phenomena by seeing them in the light of their development. And thus we find, Comte tells us, a confirmation of the chief intellectual character of the new science — the philosophical preponderance of the spirit of the whole over the spirit of detail.

A few last words by Comte on method are in order here since they relate conspicuously to the present penchant for mathematical exactitude. They go as follows: "The most perfect methods may, however, be rendered deceptive by misuse and this we must bear in mind. We have seen that mathematical analysis itself may betray us into substituting signs for ideas, and that it conceals inanity of conception under an imposing verbiage."

## The Religion of Humanity

Comte's Positive Polity spells out the positivist religion which came to serve as the Bible for a rather odd collection of worshippers. Despite his attempt to replace all existing beliefs, customs, and conventions by new names, Comte's bizarre religion still retained old ideas and sentiments. Thus, the little French boy who had broken away from Catholicism and denounced the theological method of thought (but not religion) wound up by founding a church of his own.

His church, founded on the Religion of Humanity, was a strange concoction. Sociologists were to be its priests. They were to be the scientific directors of society and to interpret the positivist doctrine of love, order, and progress. The positivist priests were not to exercise political power but to influence opinion through education and preaching. The common man, imbued with the positivist philosophy, would thus be able to evolve a most enlightened public opinion. This common man would be a proletarian. The future belonged to the intelligent workingman, not through losing his chains but through improving his positivistic brains. Comte was seeking to compensate men for the God and the universal (Catholic) church that positivism and sociology must necessarily take from them. He also feared the triumph of the military and distrusted professional politicians although some of his political views, especially regarding the Revolution of 1848 and the Second Empire, were extremely naïve. If he did not expect that all men would, through positivism, become quickly altruistic, he at least hoped that a form of secular worship would help them become less egoistic. But he finally went so far as to develop a messianic complex in which he saw himself as a Moses leading his positivist children out of the wilderness of theology and metaphysics to a land flowing with milk, honey, and sociology. It sounds like premature senility unless one tears away the elaborate trappings and sees underneath them the sublimation of his love of mankind, his hatred of cruelty, and his worship of women.

There is a school of thought in France which holds that there is no inherent contradiction between the scientific Comte who founded sociology, classified and interrelated the sciences, and propounded the law of the three stages, and the later Comte who founded the Religion of Humanity since, it is claimed, in both cases his ruling passion was the betterment of man. Comte was not willing to accept the possibility that a strong sense of selfhood could be sufficiently established in men without rites, ceremonials, daily worship, and collective institutions such as his new religion demanded and without a new universal group such as his positivist church.

# 7

# Herbert Spencer and the Evolutionary Defense of Individualism

## 1. General Nature of Spencer's Philosophical and Sociological System

### A. Life and Works

Comte's work in the field of sociology was taken up and greatly amplified by the philosopher who, better than anyone else, summed up the main currents of the nineteenth-century social thought, Herbert Spencer (1820–1903). This does not mean that Spencer regarded Comte as his scientific precursor. In fact, quite the opposite was the case, for Spencer published his first sociological treatise, *Social Statics*, before he had any knowledge of Comte's ideas, and it seems that in many respects the similarity between the two writers was accidental. On the other hand, it is hard to agree entirely with Spencer in his attempt to prove his complete independence of Comte and his fundamental divergence from the views of the latter.[1] Rather, it would be almost as accurate to accept the verdict of Henri Michel: "It does not follow that the *Principles of Sociology* can actually be regarded as an original book by anyone who has read the *Opuscules* (i.e., the early essays) of Comte. All the leading ideas, even in the method, of Spencer are to be seen in the *Opuscules*. Comte traced the outlines: Spencer only filled them in."[2]

A child of feeble health, Spencer was taught at home and never received any public education. In this aspect of home training he resembled his famous contemporary, John Stuart Mill. His failure to follow a university career doubtless tended to contribute strongly to the refusal of formal academic circles in England to take a lively interest in Spencer's teachings; and his lack of a properly socialized existence in early life

From Harry Elmer Barnes, ed., *An Introduction to the History of Sociology* (Chicago: The University of Chicago Press, 1970), pp. 110–137, by permission of the publisher.

certainly had not a little to do with his individualistic tendencies as an adult. Aside from these more strictly personal elements, Spencer's non-conformist inheritance from his family and his reaction against the radical revolutionary doctrines of his youth are matters which must be taken into consideration when attempting to get an insight into the sources of his philosophic tendencies and an understanding of his intellectual predispositions.[3]

Spencer early acquired a taste for mechanics, and in 1837 he became chief engineer of the London and Birmingham Railroad. He resigned from this position in 1848 to become subeditor of the *Economist*; and during the four years that he served in this capacity he produced (1850) his first important contribution to sociology, *Social Statics*. During the next eight years he developed the basic principles of his system of synthetic philosophy and published them in the *First Principles* in 1863. No one can understand Spencer's philosophy if he has not read this work, anymore than one can appreciate Comte's fundamental ideas if one has not read his early essays.

In this volume Spencer disposed of metaphysical theology by relegating it to the realm of the ultimately unknowable; he outlined his theory of universal evolution; and he indicated the main lines of its application to the totality of human knowledge. He did not, as has frequently been asserted, attempt to apply the theories of Darwin to a restatement of science and philosophy. Rather, he applied to this field his own theory of evolution, which had been formulated prior to, and independent of, that of Darwin and was built upon a thoroughly distinct, though compatible, set of fundamental propositions.[4]

## B. Spencer's Philosophy of Society

This is not the place to attempt to pass final judgement upon the merits of Spencer's system as a whole. It certainly suggested the general line of approach to modern scientific knowledge, which seems, on the whole, essentially correct, namely, the evolutionary viewpoint, however much of Spencer's particular view of evolution may fail to bear the test of later and more specialized inductive and quantitative studies. Again, it is quite safe to say that his system represents one of the most impressive products of a single human mind since the time of Aristotle. Further, there can be little doubt that, for innate mental productivity, Spencer is quite unequaled among modern writers. It requires a remarkable man, for instance, to produce Wundt's treatises on psychology, in which the author seems to have had a good acquaintance with every important work on his special subject. But, though such a work may be infinitely more valuable from a scientific point of view, it requires less genius to produce it than it did for Spencer to create the *Principles of Psychology* from the recesses of his own mind, after having read less formal psychology than the average elementary-school teacher in an American public school.

In short, whatever in Spencer's system may be destroyed by subsequent scientific progress — and it seems that much of it has even now passed into the realm of rhetoric — still he may claim the distinguished honor of having placed nearly all the phases of scientific study upon the road to further progress by making their guiding principle the concept of evolution. The late William Graham Sumner has well stated the significance of Spencer's establishment of the evolutionary principle in social science:

> Mr. Spencer addressed himself at the outset of his literary career to topics of sociology. In the pursuit of those topics he found himself forced to seek constantly more fundamental and wider philosophical doctrines. He came at last to the fundamental principles of the evolution philosophy. He then extended, tested, confirmed, and corrected these principles by inductions from other sciences, and so finally turned again to sociology, armed with the scientific method which he had acquired. To win a powerful and correct method is, as we all know, to win more than half the battle. When so much is secure, the question of making discoveries, solving the problems, eliminating the errors, and testing the results, is only a question of time and of strength to collect and master the data.[5]

The natural and social sciences were thus rescued from the retrospective and obscurantic tendencies with which they had been struggling more or less hopelessly ever since patristic theology had shackled induction and empiricism by reliance upon ecclesiastical authority and justification by faith and by opposition to the discovery of any scientific facts subversive of the tenets of accepted "truth."[6]

As Spencer's whole system of social science was built upon his general laws of evolution, it is essential to understand the fundamental propositions involved in his doctrines on this point. This is incomparably more important in Spencer's sociology than in his development of the organic analogy, though most expositors and critics of his sociology have dwelt mainly upon the later.

Spencer's laws of universal evolution are found in their complete development in the second part of his *First Principles*. In the first place, he finds three fundamental truths or propositions. Of these, the basic one is the law of persistence of force, which means the existence and persistence of some ultimate cause which transcends knowledge. The other two principles are the indestructibility of matter and the continuity of motion, both being derived from the principle of the persistence of force. There are, in turn, four secondary propositions. The first is the persistence of the relations among forces, or the uniformity of law. The second is the transformation and equivalence of forces, namely, that force is never lost but is merely transformed. The third is the law that everything moves along the line of least resistance or of greatest attraction. The fourth and final law is that of the rhythm or alternation of motion.

To render this system complete, some law must be found which will govern the combination of these different factors in the evolutionary process. This need is supplied by the law that, with the integration of matter, motion is dissipated and, with the differentiation of matter, motion is absorbed. As a result, the process of evolution is characterized by a passage from an incoherent homogeneity to a coherent and co-ordinated heterogeneity. From these foundations, Spencer summarizes his complete law of universal evolution as follows: "Evolution is an integration of matter and a concomitant dissipation of motion during which the matter passes from a relatively indefinite, incoherent homogeneity to a relatively coherent heterogeneity and during which the retained motion undergoes a parallel transformation."

When we add to this basic foundation of his evolutionary system such important corollaries as the instability of the homogeneous, due to the incidence of unlike forces; the spread of differentiating factors in a geometrical ratio; the tendency of differentiated parts to become segregated through a clustering of like units; and the final limit of all the processes of evolution in an ultimate equilibrium, Spencer's system of evolution stands complete in outline. As the reverse of evolution stands dissolution, in which the achievements of evolution are undone through a reversal of the stages in the process.[7]

Spencer briefly applied this evolutionary formula to all phenomena in the remaining portion of his *First Principles,* and the application to social processes therein to be found is the vital portion of Spencer's sociological system. The detailed expansion of this preliminary outline found in the *First Principles* constitutes Spencer's system of "Synthetic Philosophy."

Spencer's formal treatment of sociology, aside from the outline of his system in the *First Principles*, is to be found in the *Study of Sociology* — a sort of prolegomenon to the subject and still an indispensable introduction — and in the three large volumes of the *Principles of Sociology*. While Spencer gave an excellent summary of his whole philosophical system, he failed to present a succinct digest of his sociological theory. Professor Giddings attempted to supply this need and performed the task in a manner satisfactory to Spencer. His lucid and comprehensive summary follows:

Societies are organisms or they are super-organic aggregates.

Between societies and environing bodies, as between other fine aggregates in nature, there is an equilibrium between society and society, between one social group and another, between one social class and another.

Equilibrium between society and society, between societies and their environment, takes the form of a struggle for existence among societies. Conflict becomes an habitual activity of society.

In this struggle for existence fear of the living and of the dead arises. Fear of the living, supplementing conflict, becomes the root of political control. Fear of the dead becomes the root of religious control.

Organized and directed by political and religious control, habitual conflict becomes militarism. Militarism moulds character and conduct and social organization into fitness for habitual warfare.

Militarism combines small social groups into larger ones, these into larger and yet larger ones. It achieves social integration. This process widens the area within which an increasingly large proportion of the population is habitually at peace and industrially employed. Habitual peace and industry mould character, conduct, and social organization into fitness for peaceful, friendly, sympathetic life.

In the peaceful type of society coercion diminishes, spontaneity and individual initiative increase. Social organization becomes plastic, and individuals moving freely from place to place change their social relations without destroying social cohesion, the elements of which are sympathy and knowledge in place of primitive force.

The change from militarism to industrialism depends upon the extent of the equilibrium of energy between any given society and its neighboring societies, between the societies of any given race and those of other races, between society in general and its physical environment. Peaceful industrialism cannot finally be established until the equilibrium of nations and of races is established.

In society, as in other finite aggregates, the extent of the differentiation and the total complexity of all the evolutionary processes depend upon the rate at which integration proceeds. The slower the rate the more complete and satisfactory is the evolution.[8]

Better known than Spencer's interpretation of society in terms of the laws of evolution, though not so vitally connected with his system, is his development of the analogy between society and an organism. This analogy was by no means original with Spencer, as it is to be found in Plato, Aristotle, Paul, and many of the early Christian Fathers. It was common throughout the Middle Ages and had later been considerably elaborated, among others by Comte, Krause, and Ahrens. It was reserved for Spencer, however, to present the first systematic development of the theory.[9]

Spencer enumerates six fundamental similarities between society and organism. First, both differ from inorganic matter through an augmentation of mass and visible growth during the greater part of their existence. Second, as both increase in size, they increase in complexity of structure. Third, progressive differentiation of structure in both is accompanied by a like differentiation of functions. Fourth, evolution establishes in both society and animal organisms not only differences, but definitely related differences, of such a character as to make both possible. Fifth, the analogy between society and an organism is still more evident when it is recognized that, conversely, every organism is a society. Finally, in both society and the organism the life of the aggregate may be destroyed, but the units will continue to live on for a long time.

On the other hand, there are three important differences to be noted between society and the organism. In the first place, whereas in the individual organism the component parts form a concrete whole and the living units are bound together in close contact, in the social organism the component parts form a discrete whole and the living units are free and more or less dispersed. Again, and even more fundamental, whereas in the individual organism there is such a differentiation of functions that some parts become the seat of feeling and thought and others are practically insensitive, in the social organism no such differentiation exists; there is no social mind or sensorium apart from the individuals that make up the society. As a result of this second difference, there is to be observed the third distinction, namely, that, while in the organism the units exist for the good of the whole, in society the whole exists for the good of the members.[10]

Another important phase of Spencer's biological interpretation of society was his famous theory of population trends, first set forth in 1852. He maintained that there is a fundamental antagonism between "individuation" and "genesis." As civilization became more complex, an ever larger portion of the available physiological energy of the race is exhausted in the activities associated with personal development and expression. Hence less energy remains available for reproductive interests and activities. In short, advanced and mature civilizations seem to be unfavorable to high fecundity. This doctrine was an implied criticism of Malthusianism. Adopted by Henry C. Carey in the United States, it was exploited to counteract the pessimism of the social philosophy of Malthus and the Classical Economists.

These two fundamental theories of society — the evolutionary and the organic — comprise the major theoretical contributions of Spencer to sociology. His remaining voluminous works on sociology are primarily descriptive, though in many cases they present a keen analysis of social processes.

Just how Spencer's sociological system will rank in the future, when more refined statistical and ethnological studies permit the general body of sociological theory to assume something like a final form, it is difficult to say. It seems safe to hold that, as a physical interpretation of society, his system will remain, in general outline, the final statement of the subject. The organic analogy will doubtless be accepted as an interesting bit of figurative description but will be discarded as possessing little value as an explanation of social processes. How much will remain of his historical sociology can hardly be estimated at present. Already the researches of the more critical ethnologists, like Professor Ehrenreich in Germany, Professors Durkheim, Hubert, and Mauss in France, Professors Rivers and Marett in England, and Professor Boas and his disciples in America, have challenged in drastic fashion the almost mechanical evolutionary systems of the classical school of anthropology, of which Spencer was one of the most thoroughgoing exponents. One can no longer hold with Professor T. N. Carver that not to have read Spencer's *Principles of Sociology* imposes a handicap greater than would result from the neglect of any other treatise.[11] Still it will probably be accurate to say that, viewed from the standpoint of the historical development of sociology, Spencer's contribution was one of the most far-reaching in its influence that has yet been made. Professor A. W. Small has admirably summarized the significance of Spencer's position, particularly as set forth in the *Principles of Sociology*:

Spencer's scheme is an attempt to give name, and place, and importance to the meaning factors in human association. It is not a system of speculative conceptions. It is an attempt to represent in language the literal facts of society in the relations in which they actually occur in real life. It is a device by means of which, in proportion as it is adapted to its purpose, we should be able more truly, more comprehensively, and more profoundly to understand, for instance, the life of the people in the United States, than we could without the aid of such description. The fair test is, not to ask whether this scheme leaves nothing in the way of social exposition to be desired, but whether it lays bare more of essential truth about society than is visible without such an interpretation; not whether there is a remainder to be explained, but whether more appears in the confusion of everyday life than is discovered before it is seen in terms of these symbols. Judged by this test the Spencerian scheme is certainly an approach to truth.[12]

## II. Spencer's Leading Social and Political Theories

### A. The Relation of Sociology to Political Science and the Study of the State

As regards the relation of sociology to political science, Spencer differed from Comte in holding that the special social sciences are distinct, but co-ordinated, branches of sociology and that, as such, they are legitimate bodies of science. However, his differentiation between the scope of sociology and that of the special social sciences was not clearly worked out. His summary of the relation of sociology to political science and of the legitimate treatment of political problems by sociology, as presented in his chapter on "The Scope of Sociology" in the *Study of Sociology*, covered completely the field now generally allotted to political science, though with a distinctly sociological orientation. He says here:

Sociology has next to describe and explain the rise and development of that political organization which in several ways regulates affairs, which combines the actions of individuals for purposes of tribal or national offense or defense; and which restrains them in certain of their dealings with one another, as also in certain of their dealings with themselves. It has to trace the relations of this coordinating and controlling apparatus, to the area occupied, to the amount and distribution of population, and to the means of communication. It has to show the differences of form which this agency presents in different social types, nomadic and settled, militant and industrial. It has to describe the changing relations between this regulating structure which is unproductive, and those structures which carry on production. It has also to set forth the connections between, and the reciprocal influences of, the institutions carrying on civil government, and other governmental institutions simultaneously developing the ecclesiastical and the ceremonial. And then it has to take account of those modifications which persistent political restraints are ever working in the character of the social units, as well as the modifications worked by the reaction of these changed characters on the political organization.[13]

This is an excellent outline of what might constitute a sociological survey, if not a complete sociological theory, of the state. Spencer's fulfillment of this task in the section of his *Principles of Sociology* dealing with "Political Institutions" and in numerous essays and parts of other works was doubtless one of the most extensive treatments of political problems that any sociologist, with the possible exception of Gumplowicz and Ratzenhofer, has attempted.

### B. Fundamental Political Concepts and Definitions

Spencer seems to have distinguished in a fairly definite manner between the concepts of society and of state, though he makes no attempt at a formal treatment of this somewhat academic subject. He unquestionably regards the state as society, politically organized. He conceives of the state as that conscious organization of co-operative activity in a society which concerns the group as a whole. "Political organization," he says, "is to be understood as that part of social organization which consciously carries on directive and restraining functions for public ends."[14]

Thus, Spencer does not make the state coextensive with society or a further refinement of society but simply regards it as society when organized as a political unit. Society, as a whole, is supported by two types of co-operation: spontaneous private co-operation, which is concerned with matters that do not affect the group as a unit except in indirect ways; and the "consciously devised" co-operation which deals with the public activities of the group as a totality. It is only the latter that directly creates and supports the state.

He does not, however, distinguish so clearly between the state and the government — something that is hard for an Englishman to do, since in England legal sovereignty and the lawmaking power reside in the same body. At the same time, it seems reasonably clear that Spencer would have defined government as the particular form which the political organization may assume at any time or place, in other words, the correct notion of the government as the mechanism of administration. Speaking in terms of the organic analogy, the state is the system which has for its function the regulation of the social organism; the organs which perform this function are known as the "government." As to the distinction between the terms "state" and "nation," it seems that Spencer used the word "nation" as meaning the state in its objective political and geographic aspects — the conventional use of the term, though not the connotation given to it by the strict terminology of political science.

Spencer agrees with the usual conception as to what constitutes the fundamental attributes of the state, so far as territory, population, and governmental organization are concerned, but he balks at the notion of an unlimited sovereign authority. To an arch-individualist like Spencer, the conception of an irresistible power in society, against which the individual had no legal right of resistance, was most repugnant. Hobbes, Bentham, and Austin are as scathingly attacked by Spencer as Blackstone was by Bentham: "Analyze his assumption, and the doctrine of Austin proves to have no better basis than that of Hobbes. In the absence of admitted divine descent or appointment, neither single-headed ruler nor many-headed ruler can produce such credentials as the claim to unlimited sovereignty implies."[15]

Natural or, perhaps better, individual rights rather than sovereignty were the cornerstone of Spencer's political theory. But individual rights, as conceived by Spencer, are neither those which are assumed by metaphysical ethics nor those artificial rights conferred by a governmental agent. They are those indispensable rights which must be guaranteed to an individual so that society may exist and function properly. Such a doctrine of natural rights is perfectly valid and is not, as Ernest Barker intimates, entirely incompatible with the doctrine of a social organism. It is chiefly the excessive extent of these natural rights insisted upon by Spencer which may be called in question rather than the theoretical aspects of the problem.

### C. The Foundations and Justification of Political Authority

The question of the state and the government Spencer treats both analytically and historically. In both senses the immediate basis of political control and that which had made its existence possible through the ages is the "fear of the living," in the same way that the "fear of the dead" is the foundation of religious control.[16] Of course, this fundamental distinction is not perfect, for in some cases political control is furthered by the fear of the dead, as when a chief is believed to be able to control the ghosts of his ancestors; and likewise, the fear of the existing ecclesiastical hierarchy is an important element in effective religious control. But, in general, this must be admitted to be a valid principle of differentiation.

In an analytical sense the state and the government arise because society cannot function adequately without them. A society is not established by the mere physical contiguity of a mass of individuals. It is constituted only when there is an organized system of co-operation among these units. The state and government not only supply one of the two great types of co-operation, that which controls the group as a whole in relation to public ends, but they also promote the development of private co-operation. They eliminate the conflict among individuals and increase the size of the group in which co-operation may exist. The larger the group, the greater the amount of division of labor and specialization that is possible. In like manner, legal rights and their enforcement find their philosophical justification in the fact that only under political protection can society continue its existence and function properly. Speaking in terms of the organic analogy, the explanation of the state is identical in principle, since in any perfected organism there must be a potent regulating system in order to insure the proper functioning of the sustaining and distributing systems.

The structure of government, similarly, is easily amenable to analysis. There is a natural triune structure, due to the inherent differences in mankind. Whether one examines a primitive tribe or a modern state, the organization for governmental purposes falls into three classes: (1) the *leader*: (2) the small minority of able and distinguished men, i.e., the *consulting* body; (3) the vast mass of inexperienced and mediocre citizens, who simply listen to, and agree with or dissent from, the acts and opinions of the leader and the council, i.e., the *representative body*. Despotism, oligarchy, and democracy simply reflect the undue prominence of one of these three components of government. The great force lying behind political power and the particular structures through which it is manifested is "the feeling of the community." This is based, to a certain degree upon the reaction of the community to present problems, but it depends to a far greater extent upon the social heritage which is crystallized into custom and tradition. Political organization is simply the public agency for applying this "feeling of community." This unconscious fear of the dead (the "dead hand"), which is the psychological content of custom, thus aids the fear of the living in maintaining political control. This notion Spencer sums up in the following manner:

We are familiar with the thought of the "dead hand" as controlling the doings of the living in the use made of property; but the effect of the "dead hand" in ordering life at large through the established political system is immeasurably greater. That which, from hour to hour in every country, governed, despotically or otherwise, produces the obedience making political action possible, is the accumulated and organized sentiment felt towards inherited institutions made sacred by tradition.[17]

### D. The Historical Evolution of Social and Political Institutions

Spencer's account of the historical evolution of social and political organization is very elaborate, but his conclusions are open to the same degree of skepticism as is his generalized account of the evolution of institutions. His method was one — that of the classical anthropologists — which is now abandoned by most scholarly and critical ethnologists at the present time. From his voluminous *Descriptive Sociology* he would gather together illustrative material bearing upon the evolution of any particular institution, regardless of the relation of that particular practice to the whole cultural complex of the social groups from which the information was drawn or of the different stages of culture which contributed evidence in support of his thesis. The Shoshonean Indians and the Italian cities at the time of the Renaissance might thus be offered as supporting evidence for a particular process or "stage" in social evolution. The mass of material offered to the reader, its seeming comprehensiveness, as apparently drawn from all parts of the world and from all ages, and the incomparable logic and skill with which Spencer marshaled his evidence, all tended for years to make Spencer's historical sociology the *sine qua non* of the subject.[18]

The application of more refined methods in ethnology and the cumulative evidence from intensive original investigation of cultural areas by competent ethnologists have, however, tended to call in question many of Spencer's generalizations. Aside from his faulty methodology, the general assumptions of the classical school of anthropology, of which he was a prominent member, regarding the universality of cultural traits and the orderly progress of institutional evolution have been seriously challenged by later investigations. It is now rather generally conceded by ethnologists that it requires about four specialists competently to investigate any particular cultural area, to say nothing of attempting to survey the whole course of social evolution. An accurate historical sociology can be written only in that distant future when reliable monographs by specialists have summarized what ethnologists and cultural historians have discovered regarding particular areas and special periods. Nevertheless, it is doubtful whether anyone could have reached better logical conclusions by the use of Spencer's methods, and the healthy scepticism which one may entertain regarding his conclusions should not prevent one from having the highest respect for the constructive logic and the brilliant fertility of imagination displayed in Spencer's history of society.

Spencer's main conclusions regarding the evolution of social and political organization may be summarized about as follows: At the outset, society may be assumed to have existed as undifferentiated and unorganized hordes. The beginning of public authority and political organization was the temporary submission of the group to a leader in time of war. The natural prowess of this leader in war was often supplemented by his supposed power to control ghosts and obtain their aid, thus bringing a supernatural sanction to his rule.

In due course of time, with the increasing complexity of society, the more frequent periods of warfare, and the better organization of military activity, this temporary war leader evolved into the chief or king, who held his power for life. In turn, the difficulties and disorder which occurred at the death of a leader and during the period of the choice of a successor tended to establish the principle of heredity leadership. In this manner stability and permanence of leadership were provided for. Along with this development of the ruler went the parallel evolution of the consultative and representative bodies. At first merely spontaneous bodies meeting in times of necessity, they later evolved into formal senates and assemblies.

The processes of integration and differentiation are exhibited in the development of political organization, as well as in evolution in general. The long period of military activity which characterized the earlier stages of political evolution brought about the consolidation of the petty primitive groups and their respective territory. Because the best-organized groups tended to win in the intergroup struggle, the integration of society and the extension of the range of power of the successful state was a cumulative process. Along with the integration of political authority, both in the scope of its application and in the expansion of the area of control, there went a corresponding increase in differentiation and coordination. The differentiation in society, which begins in the family, is extended through the periods of conquest that characterize early political progress, until it has created the classes of wealthy rulers, ordinary freemen, serfs and slaves. As political power becomes concentrated in a definite ruling class and is increased in scope and applied over a larger territory, it has to be delegated in order to be administered with efficiency. All the vast machinery of modern government, with its ministries; its local governing agencies; its judicial, revenue, and military systems, is but the further differentiation and co-ordination of the earlier fundamental organs of government, manifested in the simple triune structure of chief, council, and assembly.

The state, at first, centers all its attention upon military organization, conquest, and territorial aggrandizement; but, as time goes on, its concern is turned more and more toward the development of industry. From this moment onward, the process of political evolution becomes a transformation of the military state into the industrial state. This process is still under way. The purely industrial state, however, is not the final goal of social evolution. The ultimate stage to be hoped for is one in which the resources of a developed industrialism may be turned toward the perfection of human character in the higher and more truly socialized aspects of moral conduct, thus bringing into being the ethical state.

Despite his elaborate treatment of the origin and development of the different branches of political organization, Spencer nowhere gives a clear picture of the evolution of the state and sovereign power as a related whole, and this failure doubtless contributed in a large degree to making Spencer unable to grasp and concede the real significance of the state.

### E. Forms of the State and the Government

In his treatment of the forms of the state, Spencer discards for political analysis the conventional classification based upon the end toward which organized political society functions. Spencer finds that political society has functioned for two specific ends in the course of history — military aggression and industrial development. Comte had suggested a differentiation, though he had more accurately interpolated a critical and revolutionary period between the primary military and the primarily industrial eras. These two periods, while sharply differentiated in principle, tend to overlap in a historical sense. The present era, while beginning to be primarily industrial, still contains only too many survivals from the military regime.[19] Nevertheless, close analysis reveals the fact that each of these systems is characterized by a definite set of principles and produces a type of character in its citizens which is almost diametrically opposed to that which is found in the other.

In the militant type of society, unified action is necessary, and all must take their part in this activity. All the energies of the society are devoted to the furthering of military efficiency, since those who cannot fight are busily engaged in providing supplies for the warrior class. The individual is thus completely subordinated to society through the despotic governmental organization which is essential to produce this highly specialized adjustment of society to military activity.

To secure a proper administration of this despotic control over a large area and a considerable population, there must be a thorough regimentation of society, extending from the ruler to the humblest subject. The regulation administered by this despotic and bureaucratic system is both positive and negative. This system of regimentation develops a rigidity in society, owing to the enforced specialization, which makes it difficult for the individual to change his place in society. In fact, the position of the individual in the military era is merely one of status. In order to secure economic independence, so valuable in time of war, the society pursues a vigorous policy of protectionism. Since success in war is the supreme aim of society, bravery and strength are made the chief moral qualities toward which the ambitious individual may aspire. A selfish patriotism that regards the triumph of the particular group or nation as the chief end of social activity is the dominating sentiment in the militant state. The deadening influence of bureaucratic officialdom lessens individual initiative, fosters the belief that universal governmental activity is indispensable, and blinds society to the conception of the evolutionary factors in progress and social evolution.

The industrial type of society is not to be distinguished from the militant solely by the amount of industry which is being carried on, as militant states may be very industrious. Neither can it be completely characterized by having as its chief end the development of industry, for socialistic and communistic states also pretend to aim at this goal. Rather, the industrial type of society is one which combines the goal of industrial development with absolute freedom of individual initiative within the limits of order and equity. In the industrial type of society there is no longer any all-pervading compulsory political activity; the small amount of such discipline that is retained is designed merely to prevent unnecessary interference with individual initiative and freedom. For this type of society a representative, and not a despotic, government is required, and the function of such a government is to administer justice or, in other words, to see that each member of society gets a reward which is directly proportionate to, and resultant upon, his efforts.

The government, instead of being both positively and negatively regulative, as in the militant state, is now only negatively regulative. The position of the individual changes from one of status to one of contract. Individual activity and voluntary co-operation are encouraged. Society in the industrial regime is plastic and easily adaptable to change. Finally, since there is no longer any need of economic self-sufficiency, the rigid protectionist policy must break down, and the economic barriers of nationality tend gradually to be dissolved. A regional form of government, or a federation of governments, may be looked forward to as the goal of political organization. As to the reaction of the industrial era upon the traits of society, patriotism tends to become more refined, society loses its faith in the infallible efficacy of governmental interference, and individuality becomes stronger, more self-assertive, and mutually respectful of rights. Though industrialism is still only very imperfectly realized, it should not be assumed to be the final goal of social evolution. A new era, primarily devoted to the development of man's ethical nature, may be hoped for after the industrial regime has been perfected. The final or ultimate form of social and political organization, then, is the ethical state.

Spencer does not devote any considerable space to the question of the forms of government. His detailed account of the evolution of "political forms" is mainly concerned with an analysis of the development of what are usually known as the "departments" of government. Spencer claims, however, that a close relation exists between these departments of government and the different forms of government, for he revives the old classical doctrine that monarchy is a government characterized by the undue predominance of the single leader; oligarchy a type in which the council is abnormally prominent; and democracy that in which the representative factor has become disproportionately powerful. Though Spencer grants the existence of these three types of government, he really believes that there are only two pure forms — monarchy and representative government, meaning by the latter, democracy.

Between these two extremes, which are based upon the contradictory assumptions that society should obey the will of one individual and that its members should be governed by their own wills, there are a number of different grades of mixed governments. While these mixed forms of government are absurd from the standpoint of logic, they are good enough in practice, as their incongruities agree with those of a society in transition from the rigid military state to the plastic industrial state: "Nevertheless, though these mixed governments, combining as they do two mutually destructive hypotheses, are utterly irrational in principle, they must of necessity exist, so long as they are in harmony with the mixed constitution of the partially adapted man."[20]

Democracy, Spencer defines as "a political organization modelled in accordance with the law of equal freedom."[21] Or, again, he describes it as "a system which, by making the nation at large a deliberative body, and reducing the legislative assembly to an executive, carries self-government to the fullest extent compatible with the existence of a ruling power."[22]

While granting that monarchy and despotism had their historical function, Spencer was wholly in favor of democracy in any society in which the citizens have reached a sufficiently high level of moral and intellectual development to be entrusted with the administration of this type of government. Not every society is fitted for the maintenance of a democratic government. Conduct has to be ruled either by internal or by external restraint; hence, among those people whose moral sense has not been sufficiently developed to furnish an adequate internal restraint a democracy is out of place and a more coercive type is needed. Not only must there be a high moral sense among the citizens to make democracy practicable, but there must also be a sufficient degree of intelligence and a high enough estimation of the value of freedom to make the citizens alert in detecting infringements upon their liberty and capable in use of the franchise. When such conditions exist, democracy is the ideal type of government. In no case should one put faith in a particular type of government as such. The best is out of place and likely to fail except among a people whose national character fits them by experience for such a form:

> Anyone who looks through these facts and facts akin to them for the truth they imply may see that forms of government are valuable only where they are products of national character. No cunningly devised political arrangements will of themselves do anything. No amount of knowledge respecting the uses of such arrangements will suffice. Nothing will suffice but the emotional nature to which such arrangements are adapted — a nature which during social progress has evolved the arrangements.[23]

### F. Sovereignty, Liberty, and the Sociological Theory of Political Rights

For the doctrine of legal sovereignty Spencer had little respect. The whole conception was repugnant to his mind. Consequently, he avoided any attempt to trace its origin or to define its attributes. His main concern was to dispute the tenets of the upholders of the doctrine and to establish logical and historical grounds for justifying limitations upon sovereignty.

Spencer was willing to admit that there is such a thing as what Dicey calls "political sovereignty," but he claimed that some higher justification of submission to authority must be discovered. To this quest he devotes the last essay in *Man versus the State*, which he entitles "The Great Political Superstition," meaning by this the doctrine of the sovereignty of the legislative, which had supplanted the outgrown doctrine of the sovereignty of the monarch. In order to find theoretical justification for the submission of the minority to the majority, Spencer formulated the hypothetical question as to just what type of agreement to co-operate the majority of the citizens would enter into with a considerable degree of unanimity. This reminds one of Rousseau's famous problem of establishing political authority and at the same time preserving the liberty of the individual.

Spencer finds, in answer to his query, that practically all would agree to co-operate in defending their territory against external aggression and in protecting their persons and property against internal violence and fraud. To this extent, then, the submission of the minority is valid and legitimate; beyond this point such submission is unjust and illegitimate.

A hypothetical contract thus replaces the old doctrine of an actual contract as the solution of the problem of reconciling liberty and authority. When one remembers that few of the classical writers of the contract school, with the possible exception of Locke, believed in the actual historicity of social contract, Spencer's solution does not seem to differ greatly in principle from theirs, however different may have been his deductions from that principle.

As to the vital question of the origin of the basic rights of the individual, Spencer claims, in opposition to Bentham and to recent political scientists in general, that they are not historically derived from governmental action but are really antecedent to government. They are those indispensable modes of individual freedom which have been found by ages of experience to be essential to any normal and continuous social life. They existed by sheer social necessity before any legal enactment, and the only role government has played has been to codify and enforce these rights which previously existed in custom and usage.

Such a doctrine of natural or individual rights, however erroneous may be its historical justification, is not legally inconsistent with the doctrine of the social organism. Spencer's theory of natural rights as the product of social experience rather than as derived from a priori rationalization is valid. The most cogent criticism of his theory is that what he assumed to be derived from the experience of the race was quite frequently the outgrowth of his fertile imagination concerning what the experience of the race ought to have been.

### G. The Proper and Legitimate Scope of State Activity

With the possible exception of his dogma that sound social reform could not be expected to flow from direct legislative measures, the most famous item in Spencer's political theory was his analysis of the legitimate sphere of state activity. As one eminent sociologist observed, Spencer was so busy throughout his life attempting to formulate a doctrine of what the state should not do that he failed to develop any coherent positive theory of the state. Spencer's well-known vigorous opposition to extensive state activity or positive remedial social legislation seems to have been based upon two main factors: (1) the dogmas of automatic social evolution that were current in the middle and third quarter of the nineteenth century and (2) the traits of his neurotic constitution which made the authority of the state abhorrent to him.

The idea that social development and the proper working of the social process is an automatic and spontaneous affair had been accepted long before the time of Spencer. In its earliest modern form it grew out of the reaction of Newtonian cosmic mechanics upon the social science of the eighteenth century. The English Deists and the French *philosophes* developed the notion that social institutions are governed by the same "natural laws" that Newton had shown to dominate the physical universe. Their assumption was taken up and incorporated in social science by the French Physiocrats and the Classical Economists, the latter employing it as a philosophic defense of the new capitalistic system produced by the industrial revolution. Though this conception was shown to be unsound early in the nineteenth century by Rae, Hodgkin, and Sismondi, it prevailed very generally throughout the century.

With the development of the evolutionary hypothesis, a new "naturalism" was provided. It was believed that the highly organized types of animal life had developed from lower forms in an automatic and independent manner. It was easy to postulate a direct analogy between organic and social evolution and to contend that social evolution is a wholly spontaneous process which artificial human interference could in no way hasten but might fatally obstruct or divert. It was Spencer, more than any other writer, who popularized this view of social development as an argument against state activity — a position which Lester F. Ward, Leonard T. Hobhouse, Ludwig Stein, and Albion W. Small have seriously challenged.

Spencer seems to have derived from some source what the modern dynamic psychologists would designate as an extreme "anti-authority complex." Coupled with what is known regarding his early life, especially his early domination by male relatives, and his confirmed neurotic tendencies, his persistent and ever growing resentment against the extension of governmental activity probably was personally motivated by a subconscious neurotic reaction. It must also be remembered that Spencer came from a dissenting family and was reared in that atmosphere. It seems, on the whole, that his attitude toward government must have been a deep-rooted emotional foundation, since it diverged materially from some of the vital premises of his general philosophy. This inconsistency was constantly causing him trouble and entailed considerable labor in patching up a reconciliation between his political individualism and his sociological principles.

Be this as it may, his attitude in respect to the question of state activity may quite well have been suggested, and it certainly was abundantly nourished, by the political conditions of his lifetime. The revolutionary ideas of the early nineteenth century, with their doctrines of the efficacy of hasty and violent political reform, and the great volume of proposed remedial legislation designed to solve the problems caused by the disorganization of the older social control by the industrial revolution were admirably adapted to awaken sentiments like those entertained by Spencer and to prevent them from becoming dormant.[24]

Spencer published his first essay on this subject, entitled, "The Proper Sphere of Government," in 1842, and eight years later there appeared his first substantial treatise, *Social Statics*. The fundamental principle of his work is Spencer's law of equal freedom, which is but a rival of Rousseau's definition of liberty. He contends that each individual is to enjoy as perfect a degree of freedom as is compatible with the equal privilege of other individuals. In this work Spencer states his famous theory of the state as a joint-stock company for the mutual protection of individuals and presents his catalogue of activities from which the state should refrain, with a detailed analysis of his views in support of his position. This list of interdicted or tabooed activities includes the following, some of which are rather startling: commercial regulation, state religious establishments, charitable activities tending to interfere with natural selection, state education, state colonization, sanitary measures, regulation and coining of money, postal service, provision of lighthouses, and improvements of harbors. The real duty of the state is to administer justice, which consists theoretically in maintaining the law of equal freedom and practically in protecting the life and property of the citizens from internal robbery and fraud and from external invasion.

In the *Study of Sociology* (1873) Spencer repeats his fundamental notions regarding political laissez faire, especially in the justly famous opening chapter on "Our Need of a Social Science" and the equally excellent chapter on "The Political Bias." In one passage in his *Study of Sociology,* [25] Spencer anticipates the view of Sumner regarding the "forgotten man" as the one who bears most of the financial burden of state activity and gets the least benefit from this legislation. His political theories, expressed in the *Principles of Sociology,* are mainly historical and analytical and, with the exception of the contrasts between militant and industrial society, deal only incidentally with the question of the legitimate scope of state activity. Between 1850 and 1884, when he published his *Man versus the State,* Spencer contributed a large number of articles on the subject of noninterference. These have been, for the most part, gathered together in the third volume of his *Essays, Scientific, Political and Speculative* (1891). Perhaps the most important among them is his "Specialized Administration" (1871), issued in answer to Professor Huxley's attack on Spencerian doctrines in his essay on "Administrative Nihilism" (1870). By the doctrine of "specialized administration" Spencer means the relinquishment by the government of its function of positive regulation of human activities and the perfection of its negatively regulating function. He also published a telling diatribe against socialism under the title "From Freedom to Bondage"; and the second essay in his *Man versus the State,* "The Coming Slavery," is also mainly devoted to a refutation of socialistic propositions.

Finally, in *Man versus the State* and in *Justice,* one may look for Spencer's last word on the subject. In the former he inveighs against the socialistic tendencies of the age and the attempted extension of family ethics into the field of state activity. He attempts a refutation of the contemporary dogma of the sovereignty of Parliament as the representative of the majority. His final doctrine regarding the proper sphere of government, as here stated, is that it should be limited to the provision of safety from physical assault, the freedom and enforcement of contracts, and the protection of the individual from foreign aggression, in other words, to be concerned purely with negative regulations. In the Postscript to the final edition of *Man versus the State*, he admits that he is fully aware that his theory of state activity is far in advance of his age and that it will not be adopted for generations to come, but he justifies his devotion to the cause on the ground that society must have an ideal to guide it toward realization.

Spencer has been roundly criticized by many writers, notably by D. G. Ritchie, for the inconsistency between his doctrine of the social organism and his inference that, with the further evolution of society, the regulating structure of government will gradually disintegrate. That there is a discrepancy here which even Spencer's ingenuity was never quite able to explain away cannot be denied, but the logical completion of the organic doctrine, with its assertion that the function of government must become more and more all-inclusive, is hardly satisfactory. With a type of society in which intellect guides legislation, as was assumed by Comte and later by Ward, progress might be hoped for through an extension of state activity; but, in view of the present general level of intelligence and moral character of the usual run of the governmental officers in modern political systems, many thinkers would rather trust to the efficacy of voluntary organization. It seems that this was essentially Spencer's view.

As to the activity of the state in international matters, it has already been pointed out that Spencer believed that the state should protect its citizens from the aggression of invaders. Spencer was not a believer in the doctrine of passive submission. He did, however, strongly advocate the principle of nonaggression. He believed in the principle of international arbitration and prophesied that, in time, this would be the universal mode of settling international disputes. He looked forward, in the distant future, to a general dissolution of strict national lines and the institution of a universal government or a federation of governments. Spencer followed up his belief in international arbitration by personal activity in promoting a peace society that worked for international conciliation, and he tells in his *Autobiography* of the injury to his health caused by his exertions in this field of effort.

Spencer was also a vigorous critic of the new capitalistic imperialism

which developed in England and in the world generally, following the
seventies. In one of his latest articles, entitled "Imperialism and Slavery,"
Spencer criticized British policy in the Boer War as based wholly on the
principle of superior force, which he alleged to be the dominating principle of the new imperialism. He further asserted that imperialism inevitably leads to militarism, destroys democracy both at home and abroad
and vastly increases the burdens of taxation. He thus came very near to
the position taken by the neoliberals, Hobhouse and Hobson, differing
chiefly in not complaining that the expenditures for imperialism reduced
desirable appropriations for social legislation at home.

In conclusion, it seems that whatever one may think of Spencer's
doctrine of the legitimate field of state activity, no thoughtful person can
easily dissent from the assumptions which produced at least half of his
opposition to state interference: (1) the present low level of political
morality; (2) the general lack of intelligence or, at least, of special compe-
tence on the part of the agents of government; (3) the failure of the
electorate to exercise any considerable degree of wisdom in the choice of
these agents; and (4) the present perversion of the attitude toward government as an end in itself rather than as a means toward an end. He held
that these shortcomings all combine to make our governmental machinery miserably incompetent to deal with the complex problems of modern
civilization. The improvement of this condition can be effected in but
two ways: a decrease in the activity of government or an increase in its
efficiency. The latter is held by most contemporary writers to be by all
odds preferable, but Spencer considered it so remote a possibility that he
chose to put his trust in the former. That he had some valid grounds for
his attitude is distressingly apparent.

### H. Progress, Social Reform, and State Activity

Spencer's writings on the subject of social reform are about as prolific
and spirited as those dealing with the proper field of state activity. In fact,
these questions are but different sides of the same problem. As the
foundation of his doctrine concerning state activity was equal freedom,
natural rights, and negative regulation, so in regard to social reform his
central dictum was that results are not proportional to appliances.

Spencer did not deny the need of political reform or the tendency of all
governmental structure to become conservative and to resist change. In
his *Principles of Sociology*, Spencer gives an illuminating discussion of how
political organization, like all other social institutions, tends to resist

change. It was not the need of reform that he questioned; it was, rather, the efficacy of the methods and principles of reform then proposed.

What Spencer desired to emphasize was that it is futile to expect that any measure directly designed to remedy a certain situation could be successful unless it took into consideration the general cultural complex of which the particular defect was a part and allowed for the interdependence of social forces and institutions. Writers have accused Spencer of dealing with "straight men" and formulating a "political arithmetic," but, in this field of social reform at least, he was sufficiently conscious of the actual conditions which confront the social reformer. His classic statement of this principle is contained in the following paragraph from the *Study of Sociology:*

> You see that this wrought-iron plate is not quite flat; it sticks up a little here toward the left — "cockles," as we say. How shall we flatten it? Obviously, you reply, by hitting down on the part that is prominent. Well, here is a hammer, and I give the plate a blow as you advise. Harder, you say. Still no effect. Another stroke: well, there is one, and another, and another. The prominence remains, you see: the evil is as great as ever — greater, indeed. But this is not all. Look at the warp which the plate has got near the opposite edge. Where it was flat before it is now curved. A pretty bungle we have made of it. Instead of curing the original defect, we have produced a second. Had we asked an artisan practised in "planishing," as it is called, he would have told us that no good was to be done, but only mischief, by hitting down on the projecting part. He would have taught us how to give variously-directed and specially-adjusted blows with a hammer elsewhere: so attacking the evil not by direct but by indirect actions. The required process is less simple than you thought. Even a sheet of metal is not to be successfully dealt with after those common-sense methods in which you have so much confidence. What, then, shall we say about a society? "Do you think I am easier to be played on than a pipe?" asks Hamlet. Is humanity more readily straightened than an iron plate?[26]

Nevertheless, Spencer was not a complete and unqualified advocate of laissez faire. What he was trying to combat was the all too prevalent tendency to repose complete trust in the efficacy of legislation as a cure-all for social ills. As a spirited advocate of the opposite school, he naturally went too far. What he wanted to impress upon any society was the necessarily small part which an individual or even a generation can hope to achieve in changing the direction of social evolution. He did not desire to discourage either individual or collective effort toward reform, provided that it recognized the necessary social limitations upon the scope or results of such action. He sums up this position well in the following paragraph:

> Thus while admitting that for the fanatic some wild anticipation is needful as a stimulus, and recognizing the usefulness of his delusion as adapted to his particular nature and his particular function, the man of the higher type must be content with greatly moderated expectations, while he perseveres with undiminished efforts. He has to see how comparatively little can be done, and yet find it worth while to do that little: so uniting philanthropic energy with philosophic calm.[27]

Few would today uphold so extreme a policy of laissez faire as Spencer sanctioned or wait so patiently for the impersonal laws of evolution to work out a program of reform as he assumed to be willing to do. Yet we cannot well doubt the wisdom of his advice to beware of the doctrine of the possibility of manufacturing progress by legislation that is not based on the widest possible knowledge of the sociological principles involved. This is the lesson which sociologists are still trying to impress upon well-meaning, but ill-informed, philanthropists.[28]

### I. Extra-Legal Aspects of Political Organization

Spencer offered numerous reflections regarding the extra-legal aspects of political activity and organization. It has already been pointed out that he rightly conceived of public opinion, or "the feeling of the community," as the vital force behind governmental activity which gives it vigor and effectiveness and that he believed that no form of government can succeed unless it is in accord with the public sentiments of the time. His analysis of the overwhelming part which custom and tradition play in formulating public opinion has also been described. As to political parties, Spencer held that their influence is mainly negative. They usually merely becloud the real issues in any political situation by their bias in one direction or the other.

On the general subject of the extra-legal forms of social control, it may be said that Spencer rendered a real service to political and social thought in correlating political organization with general social organization and in showing how hopeless it was for political reformers to attempt any political change or reform without looking at the state in its relation to society and taking into consideration the basic dependence of political activity upon social forces and interests. In this regard he performed the main service which sociologists have to offer to political theory and practice. The significance of this view has been well stated by Professor Small in what he designates as the central notion of the Spencerian philosophy: "The members of society, from the very earliest stages, arrange themselves in somewhat permanent forms; these forms are rearranged in adaptation to varying needs; the forms are related, both as cause and effect, to the individuals who make up the society; they are thus factors that may never be left out of account in attempts to understand real life."[29]

## *J. Summary of Spencer's Social and Political Theories*

Spencer's salient social and political doctrines, then, may be summarized as follows: (1) He revived the contract (agreement) doctrine to account philosophically for the justification of political authority; (2) he put forward a strong sociological statement of individualistic political philosophy, in which the state was completely subordinated to the individual and was regarded simply as an agent for securing a greater degree of freedom for the individual than was possible without its "negative interference" with human conduct; (3) he denied the possibility of securing social progress by direct remedial legislation (at least of the type he was familiar with) and asserted that society must wait for the automatic working of the general laws of evolution to bring about permanent progress; (4) he set forth one of the most elaborate expositions ever devised of the organismic theory of society; (5) he developed a philosophy of political evolution based upon the purpose for which organized society functions, finding these purposes to have been, first, military expansion, then industrial development, and, finally, ethical improvement; (6) finally, Spencer made the important contribution of correlating the state with society in the attempt to estimate its position and functions in the wider social process.

In short, Spencer approached public problems from the broad viewpoint of the sociologist, however inconsistent and inadequate at times may have been his application of the principles of his social philosophy to the solution of those problems.

## Notes

1. Herbert Spencer, "Some Reasons for Dissenting from the Philosophy of M. Comte," *Essays, Scientific, Political, and Speculative* (New York, 1891), pp. 118–49.

2. Henri Michel, *L'Idee de l'etat* (Paris, 1896), p. 462 (author's translation); see also Eugene de Roberty, *Auguste Comte et Herbert Spencer* (Paris, 1904).

3. For a brief statement of the sources of Spencer's doctrines see Ernest Barker, *Political Thought in England from Herbert Spencer to the Present Day* (New York, 1915), pp. 86–90. For his own account of his early years see his *Autobiography* (2 vol.; New York, 1904), I, 48–142. For more bibliographic detail on Spencer, see H. E. Barnes and Howard Becker, *Social Thought from Lore to Science* (2 vols.; Boston, 1938), I, xlix–li.

4. See A. G. Keller, *Societal Evolution* (New York, 1931), pp. 12ff. *The First Principles* was followed by the *Principles of Biology* (1864–67), the *Principles of Psychology* (1872), the *Study of Sociology* (1873), the *Principles of Sociology* (1876–96), the *Principles of Ethics* (1879–93), and *Man versus the State* (1884). In addition to these systematic works, Spencer published a large number of articles which were collected in numerous volumes of essays. For a complete list of Spencer's works, see the article entitled "Spencer" in the eleventh edition of the *Encyclopedia Britannica;* and in W. H. Hudson, *An Introduction to the Philosophy of Herbert Spencer* (New York, 1894), Appendix, pp. 231–34.

   Spencer produced this mass of material under conditions far from conducive to its speedy and efficient execution. He was a chronic neurasthenic during the entire period of the development of his sociological system, and his pecuniary resources were not always sufficient to keep his plan in a normal state of progress. The Preface to the third volume of his *Principles of Sociology*, published in 1896, which completed the work to which he had devoted practically a lifetime, sums up the·difficulties of the writer and expresses his satisfaction at his final success.

5. William Graham Sumner, *The Forgotten Man and Other Essays* (New Haven, 1918), p. 401.

6. Four good works dealing with Spencer's philosophical system are: Hudson, "Spencer"; Josiah Royce, *Herbert Spencer: An Estimate and Review* (New York, 1904); Hector Macpherson, *Spencer and Spencerism* (New York, 1900); and H. Elliot, *Herbert Spencer* (New York, 1916). An authorized and approved digest of his system as a whole is to be found in F. H. Collins, *An Epitome of the Synthetic Philosophy* (New York, 1889). Finally, no one should consider himself thoroughly acquainted with Spencer unless he has read his *Autobiography*, which appeared posthumously in two volumes in 1904, and David Duncan's *Life and Letters of Herbert Spencer* (2 vols.; New York, 1908).

7. For Spencer's summary of his system see his "Preface to Collins," *Essays, Scientific, Political, and Speculative,* pp. viii–xi; cf. also Robert Mackintosh, *From Comte to Benjamin Kidd* (London, 1899), chaps. viii–ix.

8. Franklin H. Giddings, *Sociology: A Lecture* (New York, 1908), pp. 29–30.

9. Spencer, *The Social Organism* (1860); *Specialized Administration* (1871); *Princi-*

*ples of Sociology,* Vol. I, Part I. Citations from the *Principles of Sociology* are from the New York edition of 1896.

10. Spencer, *Principles of Sociology,* Vol. I, Part II, chaps. ii–ix, particularly chap. ii. More detailed analysis of Spencer's organic theory of society are to be found in F. W. Coker, *Organismic Theories of the State* (New York, 1910), pp. 124–39; and Ezra T. Towne, *Die Auffassung der Gesellschaft als Organismus, ihre Entwickelung und ihre Modifikationen* (Halle, 1903), pp. 41–48.

11. See his [Carver's] review of the work in F. G. Peabody, *A Reader's Guide to Social Ethics and Allied Subjects,* p. 29.

12. A. W. Small, *General Sociology,* p. 130. For estimates of Spencer's importance for sociology see F. H. Giddings, *Principles of Sociology* (New York, 1896), Book I, chap. i, and his adaptations of Spencer's doctrines in all his works; Ward, *Dynamic Sociology,* I, 139–219; Small, *General Sociology,* pp. 109–53; E. A. Ross, *Foundations of Sociology* (New York, 1905), pp. 42–47; and, above all, Leopold von Wiese, *Zur Grundlegung der Gesellschaftslehre: Eine kitische Untersuchung von Herber Spencer's System der synthetischen Philosophie* (Jena, 1906).

13. Spencer, *Principles of Sociology,* Vol. I, sec. 210, p. 438; cf. also *Study of Sociology,* chap. i. Among the best analyses of certain phases of Spencer's political theories are D. G. Ritchie, *Principles of State Interference* (London, 1891); Barker, *Political Thought in England,* chap. iv; and Coker, *Organismic Theories,* pp. 124–39.

14. Spencer, *Principles of Sociology,* II, p. 247.

15. Spencer, *Man versus the State* (with the abridged and revised *Social Statics* [New York, 1892]). pp. 380–81. As Ritchie points out, part of Spencer's confusion with respect to the problem of sovereignty was due to his tendency to personify the abstract philosophical concept.

16. Spencer, *Principles of Sociology,* I. p. 437.

17. Ibid, II, p. 317.

18. For Spencer's own description of his method see his *Autobiography,* Vol. II, chap. xlvii, esp. pp. 325–27.

19. Spencer, *Principles of Sociology,* II, pp. 568–605 ff.

20. Spencer, *Social Statics* (abridged edition with *Man versus the State* [New York, 1892]), pp. 248–49.

21. Ibid., p. 105

22. Ibid., p. 248.

23. Spencer, *Study of Sociology* (New York, 1876), p. 275; cf also *Principles of Sociology,* II, pp. 230–43.

24. For Spencer's own account of the development of his political theories see his *Autobiography,* II, pp. 431–36. This seems to be somewhat of a "rationalization after the fact."

25. Spencer, *Study of Sociology,* pp. 285–86.
26. Ibid., pp. 270–71.
27. Ibid., p. 403.
28. For Spencer's account of his ambitious plan to make a study of the effect of so-called "reform legislation" during the whole period of medieval and modern English history see in *Various Fragments* (New York, 1898), pp. 136–40, an essay entitled "Record of Legislation."
29. A. W. Small, *General Sociology,* p. 153.

# 8

# Karl Marx (1818–1883)

To write about Marx as a sociologist is to be hedged in with perils. The dangers which surround an enterprise are no true measure of its intrinsic worth, and even the Grail does not always seem an entirely adequate reward to the reader of Arthurian romance. One can write of most of the "founding fathers" of sociology without too much ambiguity and with a sufficient candour and piety. One cannot write thus of Marx, for about him candour must go, so far as I am concerned, with scepticism and ambiguity. To write openly of Marx is to touch sacred things, expose oneself to the lightnings of orthodoxies both novel and venerable, and throw doubt on received opinions.

"What you adored, burn; what you burned, adore." So Christianity enjoined the pagans, and so I would enjoin, at least as far as the first clause goes, sociologists. The influence of Marx on sociology had been great and is perhaps still increasing: in my judgment he was not a sociologist, and his influence has been unfortunate. I do not deny him his greatness as one of the major pioneers of economic history and institutional economics. I could not deny his greatness in that his ideas, however interpreted, are, eighty years after his death, among the decisive social facts of our time. All I wish to do is to examine his claims to sociological greatness, to having affected the history of sociology for the better, and to being a live and good influence on sociology in the present.

To do these things I must first glance at an odd fact about the serious reputation of Marx since his death and rehearse, however briefly and badly in my limited space, some of his main teachings. Now when Marx preceded Spencer into a grave in Highgate Cemetery his fame was that of an economist. Disputes about his correctness turned on his technical

From Donald G. MacRae, *The Founding Fathers of Social Science,* ed. Timothy Raison (Middlesex, Eng.: Penguin Books, 1970), pp. 59–67. Reprinted by permission of the publisher.

economics — theory of value, of crises, and so on — and these disputes continued for a long time, but largely died out in the late 1930s. His contributions to economic history were sifted and absorbed, his contributions to institutional economics were (and are) neglected, and his great learning in the historiography of economics was almost forgotten, but is now being rediscovered.

Between about 1910 and 1950 — all these dates are arbitrary, but not, I think, useless — his fame was as a philosopher. Dialectical materialism was studied and expounded as the method of science and all knowledge that was reputable. Except in Russia this is no longer a burning topic — in any sense — and since about 1945 we have had, after Karl I and Karl II, Karl III who is, we are told, both a sociologist because of his early philosophical writings (mainly unpublished or obscure in his lifetime), and a philosopher because of his sociology. It is with Karl III that we will ultimately be concerned here.

I am not arguing that this account of Marx's reputation justly mirrors what should have been; merely that it happened, and that this is significant. It results largely, not altogether, from the investment of faith which men made in Marxism, and from the fact that Marxism was rich enough, one vein all but exhausted or shown to contain only fool's gold, for others to be explored. One could, indeed, offer a Marxist interpretation of this history, but it would not be very profitable or appropriate here.

It would be helpful had we space here to explore the personal and intellectual biography of Marx from his birth in Trier in 1818 into a family alienated at once from Judaism and from provincial German society, to his death in London in 1883 after thirty-five years' exile in an England with which he could never be bothered to identify himself, and in which he had been the pensioner of Engels — a more complex, original and deeply ambiguous man than his biographer, Mayer, suggests. In this long exile Marx played ineffectual politics, wrote an enormous amount of good journalism and excellent, savage, learned letters, and left us the torsos, the fore-studies and afterwords of uncompleted books. His work seems to me distinct from that of Engels, not always congruent with it, but yet always closely related to it. It is like the symbiosis by which one species of crab conceals and arms its claws by mounting on them sea anemones which gain from the crab's mobility and share its appetite.

This appetite was almost as universal as the nineteenth century of

which Marx was so gigantically representative. Marx could have been an
actor in the human comedy of his favourite novelist Balzac, characterized by a monomaniac avidity for knowledge, for the interconnexion of
things, and for that ambiguous power which prophetic minds possess
and which is always flawed by an obsessive need never to be wrong. But
for one thing he had no conscious appetite, and that was to be a sociologist in the sense in which the word was used by his contemporaries,
Comte and Spencer.

Partly, indeed, he could not be a sociologist, for sociology is a form of
inquiry, and he already knew. More profoundly he could not be one, for
he was concerned not with the social but with what underlies and explains the social; that is, in his judgment, with the economic order. And
lastly, he did not need to be one, for he was concerned above all with a
philosophic anthropology and his favourite tense was the future. Yet
none of this prevents the extraction of something very like a sociology
latent in his work, and though I would not entirely agree, it can be
argued that this was until recently the most satisfactory and fruitful
general sociology available. More importantly, it was for long and is for
many the only easily available body of social thought, and it carries with
it a promise of relief from the burdens of want, fear and hope, and the
justifications for wrong and error if they are committed in its name.

One can sum this latent sociology in something like the following
terms. The appearance of society is not its reality. Despite reservations
and hesitations, the structure of society consists of an economic reality
and social epiphenomena, surface phenomena which only rarely affect
the underlying reality. This basis for most of history is that of economic
exploitation of the many by the few. Politics is the violence and chicane of
the few. Religion is the sorry consolation of the many. The family is the
embodiment in little of the exploitation which is the class-system. Art is
the mask of corruption and the reassurance of the mighty that their world
is one of beauty and peace — or, Marx was a romantic and inconsistent, it
is the cry of despair from the heart of the many and the rending of the veil
of illusion by individual genius. Science is the technical basis of economic
power and interest. Philosophy is ideology — for to Marx ideology, which
had been the science of ideas, is the corruption of ideas by advantage and
desire.

Society is change. Sometimes Marx — often Engels — writes as a kind
of technological determinist to whom technology includes not merely the
material techniques of economic production, but also the techniques of

economic organization — 'the relations of the means of production.' Five great modes of social being successively embody the dynamics of society. (This is largely Engels.) First was the sparse Eden of primitive communion — a concept so odd and difficult that in a short article one must avoid it out of mere prudence. Second is slavery — the economy of the ownership of the exploited. Third is feudalism — agrarian exploitation without the burden of ownership to hinder exploitation. Fourth is capitalism with exploitation made impersonal by the market and production maximized by the machine and the routine of the factory. Fifth will be socialism, society without exploitation, without ideology, with no breach of appearance from reality, nor let to the self-realization of man.

Society is class, and class is opposition, the constant war of those who have on those who have not, the sporadic war of those who have not on those who have. But class is complex: the polarization is seldom complete, and, to change the metaphor, through its interstices new exploiting classes have emerged, the gods have defeated the titans, and exploitation takes new forms. Only with the last stages of capitalism will there be naked confrontation of the few and the many because of the specifically economic dynamics of capitalism which (1) concentrate power in fewer and fewer hands, (2) produce — absolutely, or relatively? — ever greater impoverishment, (3) result in ever more violent economic crises of poverty in the midst of potential plenty.

The consciousness of class has represented itself in many ideological forms, but in the end it emerges clearly in scientific, that is, Marxist socialism. The end of capitalism comes in a true consciousness of social and human reality — the veritable end of ideology. The mechanism of this change, as of all change, is force and revolution. Dissonance can be resolved only by dissonance. Until this resolution tension and conflict, veiled or open, are society.

Parts of this are worked out with profound research, vehemence and wit. Other portions are sketched, while yet others are briefly asserted and abandoned. There are, as in all human work, lacunae and ambiguities. And there are, of course, contradictions. It is this that has given Marxism much of its strength, flexibility and appeal as a political ideology. But this is not all.

If Marx *is* a "founding father," I would suggest the following reasons. He is deadly serious about the importance of the social as he understands it — that it is *not* the social in Durkheim's sense or, for that matter, mine, is not the point. This seriousness is necessary to any sociology, and in some ways the countervailing sociology of Weber would have been impossible without taking the Marxist seriousness seriously. To those who like or need an emotional charge before undertaking scientific work this commitment is attractive and has been important.

As I have often said, Marx stresses the non-obvious. Social appearance is not always reality. If it were, common sense and a little statistics would suffice instead of real sociology. Very often Marx is right, wholly or in part, in ascribing concealed, unconscious group interests to historic acts and professions. One form of awareness sociologists should encourage in themselves is of the covert working of interests in social relations, manifesting themselves in thought and expression.

But more specific than this admittedly important and valuable drawing of attention to the possibility of latent factors and interests in society was Marx's work on economic institutions. Here, as in much of volume one of *Capital*, he is concrete, specific and original. He stresses that these institutions have a temporal shape and his concept of the economic includes much that a modern sociologist would treat as social — and from whichever end one starts this is surely right. However one might modify or reject Marx's account of the primitive accumulation of capital or his famous section on the working-day in the factory, these remain indelibly in the mind as examples of knowledge and research brought into life by passion. Sociologists have too much neglected economic institutions. So too have economists save when concealed with their formal and/or financial aspects. To this Marx is a constant corrective. In Marx we see clearly the possibility of something better than and different from a philosophy of history; a historically specific sociology. But it is a possibility we see, a potentiality for which Marxism is no sufficient basis.

And again in Marx there is one antidote to what should be incredible: the fact that much sociology has been, and some still is, based on the assumption that harmony and changelessness are the normal characteristics of society. How anyone in the traditions of the Western world could believe this of the human condition in society is hard to conceive. Nevertheless, sociologists have apparently believed it, and at least Marx, emphasizing tension, opposition, hatred and contempt, fraud and force, and the mutability of all sub-lunary things, remains one of the harder facts of social life.

On the writings of Marx and Engels is founded most of the enterprise of the sociology of knowledge, so grand in its aspirations, but so nugatory in most of its achievements. There are other elements, consciously or unconsciously, present in the sociology of knowledge, deriving from late nineteenth century neo-Kantianism. And there is an alternative though historically related tradition in the Durkheim school which seems to me more fruitful and more genuinely sociological. For all that, the Marxist study of ideology and the work that has arisen from it on the social conditioning, distribution, and relations of ideas is perhaps Marx's most solid claim to be a founding father of one constituent of our discipline.

It is not my intention to deny that there has been a very considerable Marxist tradition of social and above all historical research, and that it has often been stimulating and sometimes convincing, or that its practitioners have not brought to light much evidence which might otherwise have been neglected. The pages of a journal like *Past and Present* in England are continuing evidence of this, and of its values. Other examples are not hard to find. This, of course, is usually Marxism in a weak, diffuse sense. For a stronger sense one is often directed to such a figure as Lukács or some more recent writers in German. About them I have reservations. And I often wonder why Marxist apologists make so little of Lenin's *Development of Capitalism in Russia* or of the learned, dull and condemned Bukharin. But none of this is to the point if one believes sociology to be possible and, in fact, to exist, imperfectly of course, for finality is not the task of true learning and science, though it is the implied claim of the Marxists.

The trouble is that the general sociology we have sketchily imputed to Marx is not true. We know too much about social structures, too much about history, too much about social change, too much — which is inevitable, but Marx *did* stake his case on the future — about what has taken place since March 1883 to accept this. We have too many workable concepts for social analysis for this system still to be useful or relevant. It is evident "that all previous history" is not the "history of class struggles," even if we interpret this as a methodological imperative: *always look for class struggle in what seems significant; all that is or was significant is class struggle.* And how inadequate are Marx's conception of slavery or feudalism, how much man experiences and devises that is outside these categories. There are social truths, many of them, in Marx, but that does not make him a sociologist. Communists should themselves perhaps be ready to accept this, and continue to reject sociology as a decadent bourgeois ideology much as they did in the brave days of Stalin. Even non-communist Marxists could consistently adopt this position.

But in fact they will not do so. Marx is one of those culture heroes who must be kept alive and up to date. For the moment sociology is fashionable because of its promise and its mystery at least as much as for its truth and its attainments. We have therefore lately had what I called Karl III, essentially a modern artifact, but more than that, for the availability of the documents has revealed a partly unfamiliar young Marx. It is perhaps not unfair to wonder why the real Dr. Marx of Chalk Farm forgot or rejected him, and to think he was right. But he, the young Marx, is now the accepted Marx except to old Bolsheviks like Kuusinen. And as I said, he is claimed as a sociologist.

Here, alas, we come to "alienation." Men are alienated from each other by the economic order—which is, of course, often true—and they are alienated from their necessary economic labour and the commodities they produce by that labour. No doubt, and no doubt by living in a world of "objectivity" we are also all metaphysically alienated. No doubt many of us would be happier were we not merely human, but made perfect and whole by some deliverance of which the proletarian revolution is but one apocalyptic instance. Religion is full of such promises. And doubtless labour is not its own reward, nor man at home with man.

But what has this to do with sociology? It is interesting as philosophical anthropology, but that is another activity. The doctrine of alienation is related to the most dangerous and least rewarding aspect of the French revolution: the terrifying injunction to fraternity. To speak very personally and seriously, I approve both liberty and equality; I regard it as an essential liberty that I am not promiscuously called "Brother." I welcome the division of labour and the diversity, even the anomie of advanced society. But in these positions I am not a sociologist, and this is not the business of sociology which is essentially the knowledge and understanding of social structures and their transformations.

At best we can find in Karl III, taking him as a social scientist almost uncontaminated by the later researches of the real Marx, a contribution to social psychology, which has some bearing, though not a central one, on the study of political sociology and stratification. It seems to me that this contribution, stressed by Lenin, was already clear from the later Marx, and that it neither greatly alters the balance sheet nor seriously offers a new orientation to modern sociology.

To those, on the other hand, who see sociology as a commitment to political action this will all be less than just. But it is not difficult to know when one is acting as sociologist, when as citizen. The knowledge of the former will often bear on the latter, and the concern of the citizen may help some in the choice of areas of social research without corrupting their work. But the two are different.

Within sociology the issues are all open, and the logic is not the either/or of Marx, but a multi-valent both/and. Sociology, *labor improbus*, has been whipped to the oar by diverse passions—generous, angry, invidious. But these passions are not its content. One does not judge Kepler by his hermetic aspirations, but his science. Marx deserves such a judgement. He has not had it, and he will not have it so long as he is thought of as primarily a sociologist. He did social research and he has inspired it. He is, as culture hero, a great fact of our age. For sociology he is, and this is not a dismissal, a most interesting historical figure.

# 9

# Friedrich Engels (1820–1895)

There is probably nothing quite like the collaboration of Marx and Engels in the history of literature or politics. Many of their works were written jointly; and, in the case of those which were not, the actual author discussed the work with his partner while it was in progress and had his approval for its publication. Moreover, there developed between them a mutual trust and respect which is more remarkable in that they disagreed with and distrusted almost everyone of their literary and political contemporaries.

It might seem that to attempt a separate exposition of the ideas of Engels is a waste of time; and it might well be if our interest were simply in the history of Marxism. In that case what mattered would be the body of Marxist ideas which took root in history. If, however, our concern is with those ideas in Marxism that might illuminate the problems of contemporary sociology, things are different. We then have to sort out some of the strands which were amalgamated, sometimes with loss of conceptual clarity, in the working political doctrine of Marxism. Even if Engels were not important in himself, it would be useful to assess his contributions in order to arrive at a clearer picture of the original ideas of Marx.

Engels was born in the German town of Barmen in 1820 and was the son of a manufacturer of deep pietistic convictions. Such higher education as he received was acquired while working in an export office in Bremen and during his year of military service in Berlin. In Bremen he became interested in the so-called Young Hegelians through reading Strauss's *Life of Jesus* and while in Berlin met many of them. On completing his military service, he was sent by his father to work for his firm in Manchester, but stopped off in Cologne to meet the Hegelian editor of

From John Rex, *The Founding Fathers of Social Science*, ed. Timothy Raison (Middlesex, Eng.: Penguin Books, 1970), pp. 68–75. Reprinted by permission of the publisher.

the *Rhenische Zeitung*, who like himself had been much impressed by the communist ideas of Moses Hess.

At this meeting, in 1842, it seems that Marx was not much impressed by Engels. He was himself a far more thoroughly trained philosopher and was at that stage wrestling with three separate philosophical conceptions: the Hegelian dialectic as mediated by Feuerbach; the theories of Hess; and the importance for world history of the new class, the proletariat, which had emerged in the French revolution. Engels probably appeared to him as little more than a romantic dilettante, not very different from other young "critical theologians" he had met in Berlin.

Central to Marx's thinking at this stage was the work of Feuerbach whose ideas he was developing in a profoundly sociological direction. It is important to understand this development in order to grasp exactly the difference which his partnership with Engels was to make.

Feuerbach produced a naturalistic version of Hegelian dialectic. Instead of seeking to understand history as a process in which Abstract Spirit expresses itself in material objects and then seeks to regain itself through human cognitive activity, Feuerbach suggested that man was the only subject of history and that ideas, including the idea of God, were simply human products. He further argued that, if man was to understand and realize himself, he must rid himself of the notion of an external and alien God.

Marx sought to develop these ideas further. If man was alienated in his idea of God, were there not other more important forms of human alienation? What about money or the state, both of which were really human creations but came to exercise an external control over man? Further, Marx felt that Feuerbach, like Hegel, placed too much emphasis upon thinking, whereas the important fact in history was not man's thought but his action. The real key to history was therefore to be found in the action rather than the thought of those historical actors who were trying to overcome their alienation through revolutions — i.e., the working class.

Marx's own thoughts on this matter were jotted down in his *Theses on Feuerbach*. But by the time they had been written, Marx had already met Engels again (in 1844) and entered into a working partnership with him. Marx had moved to Paris and had joined Ruge in editing the only edition of the *Deutsch-Franzosische Jahrbucher*. He contributed two articles himself and also included a review of Carlyle's *Past and Present*. But most important of all he received from Engels a piece called *A Critique of Political Economy*. He had already recognized that, if the social relations of production were all-important, it was vital that he should master and criticize the bourgeois theory of production. Engels now seemed to be pointing the way.

By this time Engels was busy gathering the materials in Manchester for his great book, *The Condition of the Working Class in 1844*. In doing so he met the real live proletariat in their industrial hovels, while Marx was still speaking of them as "the instrument of philosophy." It is difficult to imagine two discussions of the working class more distinct than those to be found in Marx's *Critique of the Hegelian Philosophy of Right* and Engel's book.

But the greatness of *The Condition of the Working Class* (published in 1845) lay not in its empirical description. Had Engels been merely an early Booth or Rowntree, Marx might have had little time for him. What interested Marx most was the theory which explained observable conditions. For Engels suggested that the misery of Manchester was to be explained by the simple fact of a system of class relations within which labour was sold as a commodity like any other. And he showed how this same system of class relations was leading to specific and successive stages of proletarian organization. This seemed to Marx to be the veritable "secret of the earthly family," the key to understanding social development which he had thought about in theory but could now see exemplified in history. He immediately decided to adopt Engels as a pupil who would teach him about capitalism.

The ensuing important Marxist works are *The Holy Family* (1844) and *The German Ideology* (1846). The old Hegelian Karl Marx is still to be seen in *The Economic and Philosophic Manuscripts of 1844* and in his denunciation of Proudhon in *The Poverty of Philosophy* (1847), and these works remain helpful in understanding original Marxist sociology. But Marx was excited by the new prospect of his partnership with Engels, and *The German Ideology* was intended to settle his accounts with Hegelianism and begin afresh.

What emerges in *The German Ideology*, stated clearly in Marx's letters after 1846, and receiving its fullest exposition in Marx's *Preface to the Critique of Political Economy* (1859), is a theory subtly but significantly different from that contained in the *Theses on Feuerbach*. In the *Theses,* production appears as free human activity and the social relations of production, being a human creation, are subject to human alteration. The only nature to which they refer, as Lichtheim has pointed out, is human nature.

In the new statement of the materialist conception of history, social evolution becomes part of natural evolution. The social relations of production cease to be seen entirely as the product of human agency and become instead the inevitable consequences of a certain mode of production — i.e., the particular stage of technological development. Thus revolution can occur only when the existing social relations of production are incompatible with, or 'become a fetter on,' production. The only choices left open to the theoreticians of the working class are tactical ones. The Marxist problem is to decide when technological and economic conditions are ripe for revolution.

This new doctrine of capitalist development and class struggle was worked out jointly by Marx and Engels and became the theory held by considerable sections of the working class after the publication of the *Communist Manifesto* of 1848. The *Manifesto* itself is a remarkable document which we understand too little because we have read it too much. In fact it blends the theoretical and historical ideas of the two authors and the traditions from which they came in a quite remarkable way and it contained enough ambiguity to provide a working basis for co-operation with Blanquists, Proudhonists, Lasalleans, British trade unionists and German Social Democrats in the years that lay ahead, even though Marx in his political writings might take occasion to denounce the political illusions of his allies.

In fact, the tactical compromises which Marx and Engels necessarily had to make in their political writings were not conducive to clear and consistent sociological thinking, and only the theologians of the socialist movement would wish today to take these writings as of first importance. Probably more important were those writings not concerned with immediate issues, and Marxists must be grateful that in the years of defeat and disillusion both Marx and Engels turned to theoretical questions.

Of greatest importance during these years was Marx's *Capital*. Engels had first directed Marxism into the sphere of political economy; but it was now that Marx, living partly on Engels' money, who sat in the British Museum ransacking government documents to bring up to date Engels' account of the condition of the proletariat and tortuously working out an adequate economic theory which would justify the economic assumptions on which they had worked. The first volume of *Capital* — the only part published in Marx's lifetime, in 1867 — was a formidable book, but it left a train of formidable economic problems. Its main problem was that it didn't appear to explain actual price movements or why some firms prospered more than they should have done according to the theory of surplus value. In the end it was left to Engels to edit Marx's manuscript of the third volume in which he tried to solve some of these problems.

During this period Engels completely subordinated himself to Marx, even to the extent of writing some of Marx's pieces for the *New York Herald-Tribune* for him while allowing Marx to claim the authorship and the fee. But one finds in Engels's correspondence a wide-ranging interest in religious, political and military history and a growing interest in prehistory. Perhaps one of the most important outcomes of this was the Marxist recognition of a socio-historical type called the "asiatic mode of production" which stood outside the general line of development from ancient, through feudal and capitalist, to socialist society. The recognition that oriental societies were not subject to the same laws of historical development as those of Europe was to be of great importance in twentieth-century Marxism.

Engels's interest in prehistory led him, after Marx's death, to incorporate the evolutionary ideas of the American anthropologist Morgan to Marxism. They certainly fitted well. For Morgan had apparently shown that both the family and the state were nothing other than means of defending property. It was a wonderful example of the superstructure being determined by the economic base, and Morgan's work was all the more acceptable because of his speculation that man would eventually have more than a mere "property history." Little wonder that Engels's rewrite of Morgan in *The Origins of the Family, Private Property and the State* should have become orthodox Marxist reading.

There is, too, Engels's *The Peasant War in Germany* (1850). Every sociologist of capitalist society must at some time have dealt with the Reformation, and Engels set out to assess the role of Luther and Thomas Munzer in the German Reformation. The work has none of Weber's subtlety; but perhaps that is its merit, because the political involvement of religious leaders is often pretty direct. This work supplements much else that has been written on the sociology of the Reformation and is perhaps the one Marxist study in which religion appears both as "the cry of the oppressed creature, the heart of a heartless world" and as "the opium of the people."

Marx died in 1883, and Engels was left as his intellectual and political legatee. Engels' speeches and newspaper articles gain in importance, and he remains politically active right up to his death in 1895, most notably in advising Kautsky of the "Erfurt programme," on the basis of which the Social Democratic party in Germany was to play a new parliamentary role. But of more central and long-term significance was the theoretical writing in which he attempted to sum up the method which he and Marx had been using. His *Anti-Dühring* which had been published before Marx's death and approved by Marx, went into new editions. He also worked on a retrospective intellectual biographical work, *Ludwig Feuerbach and the Outcome of the Classical German Philosophy*, and on some notes about scientific method, published after his death as *The Dialectics of Nature*. These works constitute a third Marxist philosophy and sociology which for better or worse has also become official Marxist doctrine (the first being Marx's own thinking, the second that of the Marx-Engels collaboration).

The new doctrine contrasts sharply with that of Marx's *Theses*, despite the fact that these were published for the first time as an appendage to Engels' *Ludwig Feuerbach*. In the *Theses* Marx straddled the materialist-idealist distinction and was explicitly anti-deterministic in the sociological ideas which he expounded. This is what Marx would have called "dialectical materialism" in 1845.

The "dialectic" which Engels now opposes to Dühring is nothing like this. The difference, as he sees it, between Dühring and the Hegel-Marx tradition lies solely in Hegel's and Marx's understanding of change and the laws of change in nature and society. This may separate Engels from Dühring, but it hardly separates Marxism from most modern science and philosophy. In its search for deterministic laws of progress and in its belief in unilinear development this later Marxism differs little from much nineteenth-century positivism.

Dialectics in this sense adds little to science or to sociology, and it is difficult to see why any such general philosophy is needed. It hardly helps to be told that a variety of things and processes — ranging from plant reproduction to the equation $-a \times -a = a^2$ — are all examples of the negation of the negation. And when Engels replaces Marx's definition of materialism in terms of its emphasis on "sensuous human activity" with a Dr. Johnson-like assertion that there are really things out there, we seem very far from a specifically Marxist philosophy of science.

A strong argument can be put that Engels had in fact assimilated Marxist sociology to a general materialistic evolutionary theory which was widespread in nineteenth-century England. Clearly he had not lived for so long in Manchester for nothing. But the sad thing about it all for sociologists is that Engels not merely proposes a revision of original Marxist sociology. He abolishes the need for sociology and for history altogether. The partial determinism of Marx's 1859 *Preface to a Critique of*

*Political Economy* is now complete. Man and his class struggles are all simply the continuation of nature's dialectical progression.

Such a doctrine is not of very much use in understanding either the social development of capitalism or of those forms of society which succeeded it. It could, however, provide an ideological superstructure for Marxist democrats in the west where no revolution happened, and for communist Russia where Stalin set about constructing a superstructure which would fit the process of industrialization on which Russia had embarked.

Yet to say that Engels was a poor systematic sociologist, or even that he sold out Marxist sociology to a kind of evolutionary positivism, is not entirely to deny his greatness. Marx was essentially a man of the study, the library and the committee room. Had he worked entirely on his own, had Engels not continually stimulated him by his writings and his arguments, even the rich sociological insights of Marx's early work — not to mention *Capital* — might have been lost to us; and we should not still be discussing Marxism today.

# Part III

# THE BUILDERS OF MODERN SOCIOLOGY

*T*he three chapters of Part III, "The Builders of Modern Sociology," deal with the growth and mature status of sociological theory in America as well as in Europe.

In chapter 10 the story of American sociology during the second half of the nineteenth and early twentieth century is discussed. Sumner, Giddings, Ross, and the giants of the Chicago School of social psychology, Cooley and Mead, are rightfully depicted by Abraham as being among the pioneers of early American sociology.

Chapter 11 deals with Ogburn's (1886–1959) theory of social change. His main interest related to the effects of cultural change on social change. Ogburn became widely known for his cultural lag theory, which has been and still is misinterpreted by most critics. Hence the inclusion in this chapter of Ogburn's latest statement on the subject.

In chapter 12, the Hinkles describe the general trends of American sociology since 1930s. They emphasize the increased membership in the American Sociological Association, the creation of regional professional organizations, the establishment of specialized journals in sociology, interdisciplinary research, the clarification of the relationship between theory and research, etc. All these events have contributed to a greater advance in American scientific sociology.

Positivism and social action were the two basic theories that dominated American sociologys, Pareto, Durkheim, and Weber, as well as the Austrian psychologist, Freud, are especially significant and deserve a special place in our discussion. All have had a direct influence on many of the leading contemporary theorists. The inclusion of Lundberg in chapter 12 is a tribute to the only notable American sociologist who adopted a neopositivist approach and exerted considerable influence on a generation of young sociologists.

The approach that became dominant in American sociology after World War II was social action theory. The Hinkles analyze, in some detail, those sociologists who have been "primarily responsible for the development of social action theory in this country." Specific attention is paid to Znaniecki, MacIver, Becker, and Parsons. The chapter concludes with a special discussion on Merton's contribution to contemporary functional theory. Merton's reputation among contemporary sociologists is due not only to his stress on the "middle-range theories" or his concern with the specification of the minimum requirements for the functional analysis of society, but primarily because he "has achieved an unusually successful balance between theory and empirical research."

# 10

# Twentieth-century Sociology: The Pioneers of the American School

The story of twentieth-century sociology, certainly of the first half of the century, is largely the story of American sociology. This is not to say that sociology elsewhere declined, remained stagnant or was without influence. On the contrary, as will be shown presently, the sociological tradition that was firmly established in Germany and France at the end of the nineteenth century grew and was strengthened, in Germany right up to the early thirties, and in France it never really ceased to exercise a potent influence in various areas of research, while in England certain movements, especially in social anthropology, represented a new departure in sociological understanding of immense and lasting significance. Curiously enough, however, sociology in Europe to the end of the Second World War became increasingly insulated, with the three main centres pursuing their own course with very little interchange of ideas between them. This being the case, it is not surprising that American sociology, while drawing much inspiration from the historical and contemporary movements of thought in Europe, provided in turn at most only a peripheral interest to European sociologists. So it grew and flourished independently in its own way, ultimately stamping sociology everywhere with its own imprint of positive as well as negative elements.

American sociology in the twentieth century can be neatly divided into two periods, the first of which may be called the Pioneering Period. It was a period which started with the work of the ethnographers or cultural anthropologists of the second half of the nineteenth century and continued with the work of the sociologists of the latter part of the nineteenth and early part of the twentieth centuries. Of the former the most outstanding figures were undoubtedly Franz Boas (1858–1942) and L. H.

From J. H. Abraham, *Origins and Growth of Sociology* (Middlesex, Eng.: Penguin Books, 1973), pp. 323–32, by permission of the publisher.

Morgan (1818–1881). Boas was the first scholar to have actually lived among Indians, learnt their language and written about their way of life. No anthropological research henceforth, if it were to claim any scientific validity, could fail to employ Boas's pioneering methodology or follow his example. Morgan's work, for obvious reasons, influenced a much wider circle of readers. Formulating a theory of social evolution, Morgan stressed the paramount significance of technological factors in the evolution of society. The history of man, according to him, can best be understood by taking these factors into account, in terms of definite stages of evolution through which men have passed everywhere. Like Comte and Spencer, he distinguished three main stages of cultural advance: savagery, barbarism and civilization, and each of the first two was divided into three sub-stages, all three of them initiated by major technological inventions. In this way all developments in social institutions were correlated with certain advances in technology. Morgan's *Ancient Society*, because of the crucial importance he attached to material or technological factors impressed many writers, including Marx and Engels, as being an authoritative or source work on the origin and development of social institutions. His real originality for which he is remembered today, consisted in his classification of family terms and his insight into the social significance of the language used to denote categories of kin. The lesson has only been slowly learnt that names of kin are of social origin and have a different connotation according to the social arrangement of the society in question. This is equally true of all categories of thought.

This preoccupation with primitive thought and culture was going to play a much larger part in research later on. In the meantime the vast expansion of American society in the last quarter of the nineteenth century led to an intensified interest in the contemporary American society as such. The rise of American sociology dates from this period. It drew its initial inspiration from the movements of thought in Europe. Comte, Spencer, Le Play, the German School of Psychology all provided material for what developed into a distinct school of sociology in America. Largely eclectic at first, it soon acquired an individual and unmistakable trend, holding sway where sociology elsewhere was, if not languishing, still seeking admittance into respectable academic circles.

Three influences converged to give an individual stamp to American sociology. The first was the old tradition of rural life which was being slowly supplanted by the rise of urbanism and large-scale industrial organization. This movement was accepted, even welcomed, because of its quite obvious result in the extraordinarily rapid increase of national wealth. Technical and educational resources required to meet this new phase of industrial capitalism produced that pragmatic approach to problems which was a peculiarly American characteristic and inhibited the kind of scholarly and broad theorizing by which the founders of sociology in Europe formulated their ideas.

The combination of these two factors, while producing an ambivalence in the minds of sociologists, posed a problem concerning the value system which they were determined to uphold. Since most of them came from small-town or rural areas, they could not but hold the view that the only kind of stability, order and harmony would be found in the life of a small or rural community. Hence came the emphasis in American sociology on the small group as being in itself a self-contained and self-sufficient unit of society. No other society was really conceivable, so that the same features and compositions of one will be seen to be reproduced in any number of other societies. An inevitable corollary to this view was to be found only in a large-scale urban centre. The virtues of the one and the vices of the other were wildly exaggerated. From another angle, there were not wanting sociologists who welcomed the advent of industrial capitalism, with all its attendant and acknowledged evils, as a confirmation of a species of natural selection operating in human society whereby might, in this case wealth, is not only right but is the only good.

A third influence, absent in the older European societies, made an indelible mark on American society. The ubiquitous immigrant was the new and disturbing phenomenon. He was the outsider, the stranger, the queer character with his strange ways and language. The problem now was how he was to be assimilated, accommodated and adjusted to the norms and values of the other and dominant society. Here we observe why and how the idea of adjustment came to play such a disproportionate, even an obsessive, role in American sociology.

## The Pioneers

We will now proceed to review the works and theories of those representatives of early American sociology whom we have described as the pioneers. We shall refer first to those who, like their contemporaries in Europe, were influenced by the fashionable theory of natural selection and the idea of progress. The most distinguished was undoubtedly W. G. Sumner (1840–1910). His chief work, *Folkways*, was a landmark in American sociology. He embraced in an extreme form the laissez-faire doctrine, quite in keeping with the anarchical free-for-all competitive struggle of early industrial capitalism. For Sumner, social development, like biological development, was blind, mechanical and irrevocable. Any attempt to tamper with this movement, as for example by government action, was useless and against the natural order of things. Somehow society always arrived at a certain measure of social behaviour by which it was always adapted to the struggle for survival. Social behaviour was of two kinds. First there was customary behaviour, largely unconscious, which was determined by the convention, usage and religion whose authority makes it very difficult, if not impossible, for the individual to resist. These customs Sumner called folkways. They become, as the second kind of social behaviour, mores, or morals, when people begin to think about them consciously. In this respect, morals are really rationalizations of customs, and it is this kind of morality which holds a group together and which determines what is good or bad, right or wrong. There are as many moralities as there are groups and the group which triumphs over another can claim that its morality is superior.

No other sociologist had such an extreme and inhuman approach to society. Others expressed the view that there was, after all, a place for governmental action to deal with the possible effects of unrestrained competition. Nevertheless behind all these views was the implicit or explicit assumption that some societies were superior to others by reason of their wealth and power. Such unquestioned superiority entitles them to lay down the rules for others and serve as an example for emulation and imitation. F. L. Ward (1841–1913) was a typical representative of this mode of thought. Ward introduced a large number of neologisms in his works, with the result that these have remained largely unread. He was greatly influenced by both Comte and Spencer, but what was most interesting in his sociology was the place it accorded to the social processes of conflict and opposition. If these are endemic it is also necessary to resolve them. Society cannot function or survive without a measure of compromise and cooperation. In a developed society there is a dual process of work, that of differentiation and homogeneity, to use Spencer's terminology, co-existing together in perfect adjustment. The United States is the greatest example of this and can be regarded as the model of world history.

A. W. Small (1854–1926) was less original than these two writers, and lacked their flamboyance; yet no man contributed more than he towards establishing sociology as an on-going academic discipline in America.

Small founded the first department of sociology at the University of Chicago. In 1895 he founded the *American Journal of Sociology*, and he helped to found in 1905 the American Sociological Society. What is more, Small was one of the foremost exponents of the view that sociology, concerned as it is with the problems of society, must also point the means by which these problems are to be solved. In one form or another, this advocacy of social meliorism was a marked feature of the writings of most of the early American sociologists. This was only to be expected in view of the many serious problems attending the vast expansion which was overtaking American society.

At first, Small held the view, following Comte's idea of static sociology, that sociology was the study and analysis of social structures and functions. He soon abandoned this view in favour of a more dynamic concept directed to a broad-based and historical study whose aim was the understanding of the process of social development and change. In such a study, the interrelations of various social groups and the class struggle would figure prominently. This would eventually — an almost marxian prophecy, but without the revolutionary element — lead to change in social policy towards the achievement of a more equitable social order. Like his contemporaries and successors, Small regarded the group as the unit on which sociological interest is focused.

One question, however, was left unanswered. What was the factor which brought individuals together in social groups? In Europe, the Hegelians, the Marxists, the French sociologists came out with different views. The first American sociologist to provide an original answer based on a psychological theory was F. H. Giddings (1855–1931). Drawing largely on Adam Smith's famous theory of sentiments, Giddings developed his own theory of the 'consciousness of kind.' It is thanks to this factor, by which people recognize that they are of the same kind and therefore belong together, that they merge into an organized social unit. Rather than take some of the determinants of society which could presumably be responsible for the organization and cohesion of social units, property or lack of it, religion, language and so forth, Giddings, faithful to the evolutionary and biological analogies of his day, attempted to trace the stages of this development from the early instinctive periods of the childhood of the race to finally the norms of society which demand obedience and conformity. In doing this, Giddings virtually ceased to employ his valuable concept of the consciousness of kind in any meaningful way, for it was impossible by its means to account for the existence of norms, much less for the process whereby these norms undergo a change. So Giddings's sociology resolved itself finally into a hotch-potch of crude speculations and equally crude rationalizations. For him, as for Ward, society must go through the phases of competition and struggle for survival to arrive at tolerance and cooperation. Discipline is required to maintain social life, and therefore a body of people must arise in society to see that this discipline is upheld. This immediately leads to the view that there is constantly forming in society an elite which Giddings called a "protocracy," composed of individuals who by virtue of their superior endowments are acknowledged and function as leaders of society. Here once again the more efficient and therefore the morally superior individual needs no justification, as he is a resounding confirmation of the universally established law of the survival of the fittest.

Other aspects of Giddings's sociology had a more lasting effect. He was one of the first advocates of the view that sociology is a science whose methods must be statistical; also that sociology must be psychologized without its being reduced to psychology. Henceforth American sociology could not be completely divorced from what has come to be known as "social psychology," and the development of this branch of sociology owes much to the latter work of American sociologists.

Giddings's work may be said to represent an intersection of two trends of thought, one that was slowly receding into the background, consisting of half-baked ideas, speculations and biological analogies, the other more forward-looking, determined to see sociology firmly based on sound theoretical and empirical foundations. Matters in which individuals and groups were involved were thought to be eminently qualified to be brought under observation and tested. Their interactions and the resultant pattern of behaviour would be seen to spring from some fundamental human or psychological process which it is the business of sociology to bring to light. If American sociology can be characterized by one unmistakable feature, it is its effort to bring together, and weld into one, the psychological and sociological. If, as will be shown in the course of the exposition, it had to pay a heavy penalty for this, its success in this matter, nevertheless, was remarkable.

Three people were mainly responsible for this new orientation. The first was E. A. Ross (1866–1951), who first used the term "social psychology," in the title of one of his books. Ross was an unusual character. He was a sociologist, social reformer and a roving journalist. Among the social problems he dealt with were family, labour, big business, the press and over-population. He found problems everywhere, in Mexico, India and China, on all of which he wrote with perspicacity, sympathy and indignation. As a result of a visit he paid to Russia when the revolution broke out in 1917, he published extensively on the new regime. In his primary sociological writings, he introduced a concept which is basic in sociology, viz. 'social control.' But unlike most sociologists, who have used this concept to denote the sanctions which society, whatever its forms, imposes on the individual, Ross believed that the individual himself, moved by certain inborn feelings, imposes control upon himself, from which are derived the public sanctions of the group. On this interpretation, public sanctions are a kind of guiding principle in society. Social psychology is the study of this control, and concerns itself with the static and dynamic factors which result from the psychological relationships of individuals. Ross naturally started with the view that it was instinct which brought people together in cooperation or drove them apart into conflict, but he later came to realize that this human drive, if it could ever be located, described and categorized, was the only one of the many social forces which are determined by culture and civilization. In sociology, according to Ross, the main object of study was "the social process," which was not the development of society but was itself the causal factor in all personal relationships. Ross distinguished five main types of social processes, those which might be due to external factors and those which were inherent in the very structure of society. It is from the interplay of these latter, like opposition and adaptation, conflict and co-operation, that different groups in society are continually being formed and re-formed. However crude this classification of human relationships was, in terms of pairs of polarized attitudes, it was the first of its kind, and has proved of inestimable value in having led the way to a much better understanding of social pressures.

The psychological character of sociology was even more evident in the works of C. H. Cooley (1864–1929). In one of his early works, *Human Nature and the Social Order*, Cooley expounded the theme that a man developed his individuality, his "nature" only within society. The ego, in his famous metaphor, was "a looking-glass ego," since it saw itself only as it appeared to others and in the minds of others. It was in this way that self-consciousness grew out of self-feeling. In another work, *Social Organization*, Cooley introduced and developed another concept, "the primary group," the group that was characterized by close and intimate relationships like the family, neighbors, etc. The experiences generated by primary groups were the most vital and fundamental experiences of man, and all the great ideals of life were only possible and were reinforced by the existence of these groups. As Cooley was firmly convinced that sociology was primarily concerned with group phenomena, to understand which an artist's insight and a scientist's observation are required, he viewed with scepticism the increasing encroachments of statistics into sociological investigations.

A similar approach to sociology was found in the works of C. A. Ellwood (1873–1946). Like Cooley, Ellwood thought that psychology and sociology should enter into a marriage, not only of convenience, but of necessity. However, Ellwood's interests were more broadly based than Cooley's and he was more internationally minded. He, too, held the view that the methods of natural science and of statistics were insufficient to allow a proper understanding of social life. The individual in society had a role to play in the production of social consciousness. This role can only be understood in terms of the historical background and the culture of the society of which the individual happens to be a member. Again, like Cooley, Ellwood believed in the force of tradition, of which the primary group was the vehicle. Whatever changes happen in society result from the interactions of the members of the group with each other; these interactions or relationships he called "communications," which are the most important elements in social development. Everything in society can therefore be said to be the product of collective consciousness, which is always kept alive as a result of "discussion" taking place between individuals and groups.

Perhaps the most outstanding influence on American sociology, growing with the years, was that of G. H. Mead (1863–1931). Nobody was ever able, before or after Mead, to make a real synthesis between the individual, in all his biological and psychological aspects, and society. While Mead's method was that of behaviourism in the sense that human behaviour can be regarded in terms of reactions to the environment, nevertheless, unlike the behaviourists, Mead took account of the social factors which determine the consciousness of the individual. All man's biological urges and strivings (Mead never spoke of instincts) were moulded and given shape by social pressure. Here was the first attempt made to show how ways of life are internalized and individuals become socialized. The interactions of individuals have meaning in so far as each individual plays the "role" that others expect of him. Thus, an individual's actual behaviour, including his ideas, is dominated by the social role that he assumes. He conforms to it because that is expected of him and it becomes agreeable to him because it is more or less common to the group and receives its sanctions from it.

These were the master-builders of American sociology. In respect of the number of people engaged in this discipline, and in respect of their published works as well as the new perspectives that were opened up, American sociology was firmly established with its own distinctive features and peculiar orientations. If it can be described by one word, it can be said to have been fragmentary, which was both its weakness and strength. It eschewed the kind of theorizing and wide-ranging speculations that characterized sociology in Europe, in spite of one or two attempts at formulating generalizations applicable to human society as such. It was not rooted in history, because the American system, being enlarged continuously through immigration and territorial expansions and its increasing preoccupation with new tasks, was essentially forward-looking. The practical task of ensuring the continued security and prosperity of an expanding population drawn from many parts of the world taxed the ingenuity of the leaders of society without the benefit of the advantage, which every settled community enjoys, of seeing itself as a historical entity. In these circumstances, it was impossible to expect American sociologists to look at the structure of society as a whole, to observe the interplay of forces inherent in it and the interrelations of its parts with one another.

The beginnings of American sociology, not surprisingly, coincided with that movement in American philosophy known as pragmatism. The principal idea behind pragmatism, as expounded by Pierce, James, and Dewey, is the futility of any attempt to arrive at absolute truth. Since a high degree of probability is all that can be expected in scientific matters, it is sufficient if in theory and practice we think of truth as something which works and produces the desired consequences. In other words, there can be degrees of truth, so that experimentation and innovation are the criteria of any advance in knowledge. This was in keeping with a system of social life that never questioned its basic principles, but was confident that it was moving towards a greater measure of power, control, and affluence.

Finally, early American sociology was imbued with a warm, benevolent, if hazy, kind of idealism. It felt itself involved in the welfare of society, confident in its unbounded optimism that sooner or later the problems of society would be solved. It was part of the business of sociology, it was thought, to prescribe remedies. But the sociologists were extremely vague and uncertain about these remedies. Society and its official policy proceeded in its own sweet way, conscious of its growing power, whose complacency could not be shaken even by such fulminatious and righteous indignation as the inexhaustible energy of Ross displayed.

# 11

# Cultural Lag as Theory

I shall begin with a definition. A cultural lag occurs when one of two parts of culture which are correlated changes before or in greater degree than the other part does, thereby causing less adjustment between the two parts than existed previously.

An illustration is the lag in the construction of highways for automobile traffic. The two parts in this illustration are the automobile and the highway. These two parts of culture were in good adjustment in, say, 1910, when the automobile was slow and the highways were narrow country roads with curves and bends over which had been laid a hard surface. The automobile traveled at not a great rate of speed and could take the turns without too much trouble or danger. It was essentially for local transportation. But as time went on, this first part, the automobile, which is called an "independent variable," underwent many changes, particularly the engine, which developed speeds capable of sixty, seventy, eighty miles an hour, with brakes that could stop the car relatively quickly. But the narrow highways with sharp bends did not change as soon as did the automobile. On these roads, the driver must slow up or have accidents. A decade or more later we are building a few broad highways with no sharp curves, which will make the automobile a vehicle for long-distance travel. The old highways, the dependent variable, are not adapted to the new automobiles, so that there is a maladjustment between the highways and the automobile. The adjustment, as measured by speeds, was better for local travel around 1910 than it is for long-distance travel on these roads at present. The adjustment will be better on the new express highways. Since the adjustment is made by the

From William F. Ogburn, *Sociology and Social Research* 41 (January-February, 1957). Reprinted by permission of the publisher.

dependent variable, it is that part of culture which adapts and is called "adaptive culture."

The concept of cultural lag, just defined and illustrated, was first published in 1922 in a chapter of a book on social change which carried this title, "The Hypothesis of Cultural Lag." Since I was not sure whether this term would be understood, I asked my colleague Lee McBain, then Dean of the Faculty of Political Science at Columbia University, whether he thought it was an appropriate title. He advised me not to use it because, he said, with a twinkle in his eye, it might be mistaken for a dance step. This was in the 1920s, when new types of dances in the night clubs of the Prohibition era were very popular. However, I did use the term, and I note with interest that it now appears in the dictionary and is in use in several countries in different parts of the world and has, in the United States, been found particularly useful by historians.

There is some interest always in the origin of an invention and how ideas develop. It therefore seems appropriate that I discuss briefly how this theory of "the cultural lag" was developed.

I am happy to discuss its origin, since I have been accused by some of taking the theory from Thorstein Veblen and by others from Karl Marx. I am quite sure there was no direct taking over of the idea from Veblen because I had never read him on this point. I had read Marx, and his materialistic interpretation of history was well known to social scientists and historians in general. This idea was a base, however, from which the theory of cultural lag was developed, but certainly neither the materialistic interpretation of history nor economic determinism is the same as cultural lag.

I first used the term in 1914, when I was a professor of economics and sociology at Reed College. I had for a long time been impressed with the economic interpretation of history, though as a user of partial correlation techniques I was appreciative of its limitations. The economic interpretation of history may be illustrated by the claim that the Crusades in the Middle Ages for the recovery of the Holy Land from the possession of the infidels were not a product of religious motives but resulted from the search for trade routes to the East. This economic drive utilized the religious fervor for purposes of enlistment. I do not wish to discuss the validity of the economic interpretation in this particular instance but rather to note that there was an economic factor in the Crusades and that it was obscured or disguised.

This word, "disguised," was widely current in the early part of the twentieth century because of the influence of Freud, all of whose writings I had read at the time. In his book *The Interpretation of Dreams*, he called the dream, as first remembered, the "manifest content," and the interpretation of the dream, the "latent content." Thus, if a person dreamed that a steam roller was about to crush him, that would be the manifest content, but if the interpretation showed that the steam roller was a symbol for a dominating father, that would be the latent content. The latent content was disguised. About this time, I read before the American Economic Association a paper stressing this point and entitled "The Psychological Basis for the Economic Interpretation of History," claiming that the economic factor was often disguised. But as I thought more about it, the disguise factor in social causation seemed less important than the time factor.

I noticed this time factor in unequal rates of change, particularly in the course I was giving on the family. I remarked that many changes were taking place in the family and that most of them seemed to be due to the economic factor, which removed production activities such as spinning, weaving, soap-making, and tanning of leather from the household and put them in factories, thus taking away many household duties of the wife. Yet the ideology of the position of the housewife persisted. It was said that woman's place was in the home. Also at the beginning of the twentieth century there was serious discussion as to whether women should go to college or not, because their place was in the home. I was impressed with the fact that the transfer of production from the home to the factory was precipitating a new locale for women outside the home. But there was a great time interval; that is to say, there was a lag in changing the position of women; so I came to see great importance in this lag, and, being active at that time in various reform movements, I was disturbed about the maladjustment in the position of women who were kept at home. I was an ardent feminist. So both lag and maladjustment impressed me.

I should like to digress for a moment and say that I do not consider all delays in taking up a new idea as being lags. For instance, I have been told that Queen Mary of England, who died in 1953, had never used a telephone. Well, she certainly delayed adopting a new invention; however, the failure to adopt a new invention is a delay — not a cultural lag. The theory of the cultural lag is somewhat more complex. It calls for the following steps: (1) the identification of at least two variables; (2) the demonstration that these two variables were in adjustment; (3) the determination by dates that one variable has changed while the other has not changed or that one has changed in greater degree than the other; and (4) that when one variable has changed earlier or in greater degree than the other, there is a less satisfactory adjustment than existed before.

I call attention to this series of steps in the formulation of the theory of cultural lag because it has sometimes been commented that the cultural lag is merely a concept. It is surely a much more elaborate concept than that, for instance, of primary group. I think it better to say that since it is a concept of a relationship, it is a theory. It is therefore more than merely a new term in the language.

This theory I had fully developed by 1915, but I hesitated to publish it, because I thought that theories should have some proof before publication. In order to prove a theory, one must set it up in a form that can be proved, with places for the relevant data. Thus a theory evolves into a hypothesis. But the war came along, and it was only after the war that I took up the verification of this hypothesis by considering the adjustment of law to industrial accidents, which were increasing because of the introduction of whirling machinery with rapidly moving wheels. In this case, the independent variable was technology; the machinery of which, before the factory system, had been simple tools, such as those on early farms, to which the common law of accidents was very well suited. But after the coming of the factories in the United States, around 1870, accidents continued to be dealt with by the old common law and with much maladjustment, for where workers suffered loss of life or an injury to a limb, there was little compensation and long delay in paying for these disasters to the individual or his family. It was not until around 1910 that employers' liability and workmen's compensation were adopted in this country. So that there was a lag of about thirty or forty years when the maladjustment could be measured by inadequate provision for several hundred thousand injuries and deaths to which there would have been a better adjustment if we had had laws of employers' liability or workmen's compensation.

I still considered it a hypothesis because we needed more proof than one particular case. I attempted, though, to cite many hypotheses of cultural lag, and in nearly all cases the independent variable proved to be a scientific discovery of mechanical invention. For instance, the invention of the steam machine led to the factory and only afterwards to the change in the legal rights of women. Most of the illustrations given at this time were initiated by technological changes and scientific discoveries, and the lagging adaptive culture was generally some social organization or ideology. These illustrations led to a characterization, by some, of the theory of cultural lag as a technological interpretation of history. I stated, however, at the time the hypothesis of cultural lag was published that the independent variable could very well be an ideology or a non-technological variable. For instance, changes in the law of primogeniture, an independent variable, constituted a change in the legal system and not in technology. Changes in the law of primogeniture were accompanied, after a lag, by a change in the economic system related to agriculture and household production. So the fact that the technological change came first was simple observation of a temporal nature and not inherent in the theory as such. For instance, it is quite probable that religion and not technology was the cause of most social changes in India twenty-five hundred years ago, at about the time of Buddha. Also students of Stone Age techniques have pointed out the essential conservative nature of stone technology, that it was very resistant to change, and that probably the causes of changes then were ideological or social. But in our times in the Western world, technology and science are the great prime movers of social change. That this is so is an almost universal observation.

I did attempt to generalize the theory. It is this: A cultural lag is independent of the nature of the initiating part or of the lagging part, provided that they are interconnected. The independent variable may be technological, economic, political, ideological, or anything else. But when the unequal time or degree of change produces a strain on the interconnected parts or is expressed differently when the correlation is lessened, then it is called a cultural lag. The extent of the generalized applicability of the theory rests on how much interconnection exists among the parts of culture. That many connections exist is obvious. Religion is interrelated with science. Family is correlated with education. Education and industry have connections. Highways are necessary for automobiles. On the other hand, some interrelations are slight or do not exist at all between other parts. Painting is not related to the production of gasoline. And I was about to say that writing poetry is unrelated to aviation. But I recall seeing a sizable book of collected poems on aviation. To the extent that culture is like a machine with parts that fit, cultural lag is widespread. If, however, cultural parts are no more related than pebbles strewn on the beach, then cultural lags are rare. There must, of course, be change occurring at unequal time intervals. An indication that cultural lags are common phenomena is suggested by the incorporation of the theory in books on general sociology. There have been criticisms, however.

One in particular should be noted. It has been said that the hypothesis of cultural lag is not a scientific instrument because, it is claimed, it cannot be scientifically demonstrated. The reason why, critics claim, maladjustments (and presumably adjustments) cannot be objectively determined is that there is a subjective factor which exists because of a value judgement, and value judgements are not subject to measurement.

Values are truly difficult to rank or to measure. We can measure the temperature by a thermometer, but it is said we cannot measure the goodness in morals. This observation does not invalidate the hypothesis of cultural lag. It only concerns the difficulty of determining degrees of maladjustment. But, of course, many maladjustments are quite demonstrable irrespective of the variation in the value systems. Maladjustment was an essential factor in Darwin's theory of evolution, and he had no difficulty in proving maladjustment. He used death as a test. But there are other tests. Sickness is one. So is insanity. Furthermore, maladjustment may be conceived as a deviation from a social norm. Certainly norms can be described and measured and hence deviations also. Even though maladjustment is difficult to demonstrate, and even though we fail to show it in some cases, it can be proved in many cases, and the hypothesis of cultural lag is not invalidated.

The application of the theory to modern times suggests a possible appendix to the theory which runs like this: The number of patents, discoveries in applied science, and inventions has been increasing in something like an exponential curve. Most of these are minor; but important ones have been coming very rapidly, as, for instance, the magnifying of light or the putting of vision or the isotopes from nuclear fission on tape. As these discoveries and inventions are adopted, we must adjust to them; we must adapt ourselves to this changing environment, but we do it with a certain amount of lag. So an addendum to the theory of cultural lags is that lags accumulate because of the great rapidity and volume of technological change.

However, there are certain events that tend to cause cultural lags to crumble. One of these, I pointed out in my book, *Social Change*, is revolution, and the reports we get from the revolutionary movement in China in the 1950's indicate that there are many lags having to do with the family and rural life and Confucianism that have been toppled over by the revolution. For instance, women are less in bondage since the revolution. Also, feudalism has been overthrown. An observation closer to home is that war causes a decline in the pile of accumulated lags. For instance, the war has taken more women out of the home and put more of them into industry, offices, and stores, where they tend to remain after the war is over. Similarly, the position of Negroes has been changed by war. As Negroes have been differentiated into upper classes, middle classes, professional groups, it becomes obvious that the whites cannot treat these upper-class, educated Negroes in the same way that they formerly treated Negro field hands or domestic servants. Yet many Negroes in the twentieth-century cities, with their middle and upper classes, are being treated as they were in villages of the South when they emerged from slavery, shortly after the Civil War. The war, however, broke some of the old lags because it put Negroes into association on the basis of equality with the whites of the armed forces, and the Negroes were drawn into the cities of the North. So war tends to break down cultural lags. It may preserve a few, too. This is a matter for empirical observation.

Even though war and revolution are breaking down cultural lags, there are many that persist. For instance, one such lag that is clearly demonstrable regards our foreign policy. In the eighteenth century the advice of President Washington to avoid entangling alliances with foreign powers was very appropriate because of our isolation, because of the abundance of our natural resources, and because of slow transportation. But in the twentieth century there have come the airplane, the fast steamboat, the radio, the telephone, and also the search for raw materials, which are needed for our industries and which are widely but universally distributed over the world. The old foreign policy of isolationism is a maladjustment to the changed technological situation. Isolationism, however, is diminishing. How long it may persist is a question. In the 1950s non-isolationists are the most influential in guiding our foreign policy. Yet for a large part of the twentieth century, isolationism in foreign policy was a lag.

Another illustration which, I think, is clearly demonstrable has to do with the death rate and the birth rate in their relation to the increase in population, particularly in southeast Asia. Throughout the great period of written history, the birth rate and the death rate have tended to be the same, except for intermittent periods when the death rate fell and the birth rate stayed high. When that occurred, there was, of course, an increase in population. Such is occurring now in India, where the birth rate is probably around 35 per 1,000 and where the death rate is about 25 per 1,000. The result is the increase in the population of India of 4 million per year. Occurring in an agricultural country where the farms have an acreage of about three acres, this pressure of population upon the food supply will bring hardships and may result in great human tragedies and will certainly make it very difficult for the standard of living to be raised.

This imbalance of births and deaths produces a maladjustment in other countries also, as, for instance, in Egypt and probably, if we had the figures, in China. The adjustment could be restored by raising the death rate, which of course we do not wish to do, or by lowering the birth rate, which is resisted by some moral and religious groups and by customs. However, the imbalance in the birth and death rates represents a cultural lag in some densely populated countries.

A long-continuing lag is in the adjustment to cities, which were produced in great numbers and in large sizes by the factory and the railroad. In many ways we were better adjusted to rural life. For instance, a greater death rate exists in cities than in the rural districts. There is also more crime in cities. Thus in several respects we have not adjusted well to this urban environment.

I have time to mention only one other lag, the lag in adjusting to the atomic bomb. The atomic bomb brought the possibility of great destruction to cities in a war. The atomic bomb was produced in two and one-half years. And yet, a decade later we have developed no defense against the atomic bomb, nor have we made an adjustment either in the dispersion of urban populations or in controlling atomic energy or in agreeing to ban the atomic bomb. Possibly many decades may pass before we will adjust to the atomic bomb — a lag of great danger.

If there were time, dozens of cultural lags causing very serious problems could be listed, lags which arise largely because inventions and technology have increased in volume and rapidity faster than we are making adaptions to them. The great need of our time is to reduce this lag. Cultural lags are one characteristic of the process of social evolution, which occurs in a closely integrated society in periods of rapid change. In the long perspective of history, though, lags are not visible because they have been caught up. They are visible phenomena largely at the present time.

# 12

# Contemporary American Sociology

## Reciprocity of Theory, Research, and Application (1935-1954)

The great Depression and World War II have had a major role in shaping contemporary American sociology. In general, they led many sociologists to shift attention from the task of making sociology scientific to efforts to make the discipline socially useful. In particular, these two pervasive crises influenced sociologists' participation in their professional societies, and affected the principal sources of employment, the dominant fields of sociological interest, the organization, scope, and approach to social research, intellectual sanctions, and even the theoretical developments in American sociology during the last two decades.

### Changing Professional Participation, Employment, and Interests

Membership in the American Sociological Society has been subject to extreme fluctuations in numbers within the last two decades. From its earlier peak of 1,567 members in 1932, membership declined to the low point of 997 in 1939. The 1,651 members in 1946 were the result of a slow increase during the war years. But thereafter additions accrued so rapidly that by 1953 the membership totaled 4,027.

During the years of the two great crises sociologists were frequently employed by the Federal government. Throughout the depression years sociologists joined the staffs of the Works Progress Administration, the Department of Agriculture, the TVA, the National Resources Committee, and other federal, state, and local agencies concerned with practical problems of social welfare. With the war, sociologists accepted commissions in the armed forces, participated in training programs for servicemen, became consultants or regular personnel for OSS, OPA, the De-

From Roscoe C. Hinkle, Jr. and Gisela J. Hinkle, *The Development of Modern Sociology* (New York: Random House, 1954), pp. 44–69, by permission of the publisher.

partment of State, and other federal agencies. Their professional counsel is still employed in the formation of domestic and foreign governmental policy today.

Concurrently, sociological literature and research indicate that sociologists' interests were changing. The tendency for large numbers of sociologists to forego social meliorism in the 1920s and the inclination of social work to separate itself from sociology as an independent academic department with its own professionally trained personnel during the early years of this period helped to bring about a decline of interest in social work. For a time the field of social pathology also diminished in importance, though the founding of the Society for the Study of Social Problems in 1952 suggests a renewed concern with this area. Although social psychology still remains one of the major fields, it no longer holds as preeminent a position as it formerly did. Many younger sociologists are devoting their energies to the more established areas of urban sociology, social institutions, the sociology of the family and marriage, social psychiatry, and sociological theory, and to the newer fields of social stratification, industrial sociology, cultural sociology and anthropology, communications and public opinion, medical sociology, aging and retirement, and small group analysis. These trends to some extent reflect a concern with the interactive processes and institutional structure of mass society. The small group has increasingly become the unit of investigation partly because it is often argued that prediction and control of changes in the segments or in the whole of mass society may be possible through extrapolation from small group analysis. Whatever the results, their pursuit is justified by their contribution to the development of sociology itself.

## New Journals, Regional Associations, and Specialized Societies

The establishment of new journals, regional associations, and specialized societies, although not directly related to the two national crises, reflect this expanding range of interests and professional specialization. In 1936 the *American Sociological Review*, a journal issued six times yearly, replaced the *Publications of the American Sociological Society*, which had been the official medium for the annual publication of papers, reports, discussions, and shop talk presented at the yearly meetings of the Society. At the same time E. W. Burgess became editor of the *American Journal of Sociology*. With the appearance of a new journal, *Sociometry,* in 1938, further opportunity was provided for publishing interpersonal and small group research. In 1953 revived interest in social disorganization was signaled by the establishment of the periodical *Social Problems*. Smaller regional publications were also founded during the last two decades, and in at least two instances journals with a national audience, *Social Forces* and *Sociology and Social Research*, became publication media for regional sociological societies.

In 1925 the organization of the first large regional association, the Ohio Valley Sociological Society, set a precedent followed in the 1930s by other regional groups: the Pacific Sociological Society was established in 1930; the Eastern Society in 1935; the Southern in 1936; the Michigan, the Midwestern, and the Southwestern Societies in 1937. Having a combined membership exceeding that of the national society, these regional associations permit greater personal contact, fellowship, and intellectual discussion among groups of professionals than is possible at the national meetings, as well as increased opportunities — particularly for younger sociologists — to present research reports.

Of the numerous new special interest societies the Population Association, founded in 1932, was one of the earliest. The Rural Sociological Society was organized in 1937, with its own journal, *Rural Sociology*. Sociologists and other professionals interested in problems of family life have been active in the National Conference on Family Relations, which was established in 1938. In the same year the American Catholic Sociological Society and its official journal, the *American Catholic Sociological Review*, were founded.

These developments emphasize the increasing division of professional labor in sociology itself. At the same time sociologists were actively participating in cross-disciplinary ventures with other social scientists, especially in their research activities.

### Interdisciplinary Research and Academic Integration

The two national emergencies of the period and the increasing mass character of American society raised problems exceeding the capacities of a single investigator and contributed to new departures in the organization, scope, and approach of social research. Of the large-scale research endeavors requiring cooperative effort and an interdisciplinary social science approach, three are especially notable.

The two-volume *Recent Social Trends* (1933), which involves research undertaken at the request of President Hoover in 1929 and directed by William F. Ogburn and Howard W. Odum, sought to explore the extent and direction of changes in various facets of American society. Using quantitative data wherever possible, these volumes and the related series of monographs based on this larger study report trends in technology, the economy, population structure, family life, recreation, urbanization, education, and other areas of American life. For many years *Recent Social Trends* was a standard reference work for government agencies and social science teachers alike. It remains a landmark in social investigation.

In 1937 Carnegie Corporation provided funds for a comprehensive study of Negro-White relations in the United States. This investigation was directed by Gunnar Myrdal, a Swedish political economist, and was later published as *An American Dilemma* (1944). Although the final integration of the study was the director's own responsibility, the cooperative nature of the basic research is indicated by the work of fifty-one social science advisors in the formulation of the research outline, a seven-member regular staff, thirty-one specialists who prepared separate monographs, and thirty-six staff assistants. *An American Dilemma* compiles a vast amount of historical, economic, political, sociological, and psychological data on Negroes and their relations with non-Negroes in this country. The volume is integrated by Myrdal's interpretation and supplemented by his analysis of the interconnections between science and social values. In its condensed version the work has become a standard textbook in American colleges. The original volumes are still the most comprehensive source of information on Negro-White relations in the United States.

*The American Soldier* (1949) is a summary of research dealing primarily with the attitudes of military personnel at home and abroad during World War II. Again, the several studies are the collaborative product of a number of social scientists as well as the military and civilian personnel associated with the Research Branch of the Information and Education Division of the War Department. This wartime research has certain continuities with *An American Dilemma* in directorship and financial support. Samuel A. Stouffer, who was in charge of the completion of the earlier study when the war forced Myrdal's return to Sweden, was also the staff director and major author of *The American Soldier*. Funds for publication also came from the Carnegie Corporation, operating through the Social Science Research Council. Many sociologists acclaim *The American Soldier* for advancing empirical research techniques in the field of attitude study; it is commended by others for its theoretical contributions.

This trend of interdisciplinary research was accompanied by several academic innovations in departmental integration and cross-departmental faculty appointments. The Institute of Human Relations at Yale University, founded in 1929 with funds supplied by the Rockefeller Foundation, joins medicine, law, and the social sciences in furthering the study of man. The Institute's researches, especially in the areas of child development, social and cultural aspects of psychiatric problems, and the interdisciplinary study of alcoholism are evidenced by a series of publications. In 1946 Harvard University established the Department of Social Relations under the direction of Talcott Parsons, with a staff comprised of sociologists, cultural anthropologists, and psychologists who collaborate in interdisciplinary studies. *Toward a General Theory of Action* (1951), of which Parsons is the senior author and to which Stouffer again is a contributor, aims at a unified social science theory and was written by representatives of the three disciplines incorporated in this department. The University of North Carolina has an Institute of Research in Social Science and an interdisciplinary faculty seminar under John Gillin's direction concerned with the development of the fundamentals of a behavioristic social science. Another approach to social science cooperation on both the teaching and research levels is represented by the University of Chicago's Committee on Human Development. Finally, the many interdepartmental programs and courses in the social sciences at the undergraduate level are further evidence of this interdisciplinary trend.

Funds for these large-scale integrative programs have come primarily from private foundations and Federal governmental agencies. In 1953 sociologists reported a total of 253 research projects supported by such non-university organizations to the extent of over a million dollars.

## Utilitarian Justifications of Sociology

Of all the consequences of the great Depression and World War II, none was more crucial for sociology than the change in intellectual sanctions and goals of the discipline. As the number of sociologists participating in governmental and other public agencies increased, members of the discipline reexamined the question of the relation of values to scientific sociology and began to justify the field on utilitarian grounds. In the previous period the quest for an objective science had led many sociologists to reject the doctrine of progress and to disavow reform. The promotion of human welfare and the discovery of scientific laws about social life had become separate and, in the view of many persons in the discipline, antithetical endeavors. The demand for objectivity, which accompanied the preoccupation with making the field scientific, had frequently come to mean exclusion of concern with values. While sociologists of the second era assumed the ultimate usefulness of sociological knowledge, many of them avoided direct participation in action programs because they did not wish to become identified with specific value preferences. Subsequent extensive involvement of sociologists in these practical programs, especially in the government, led to a scrutiny of the arguments about the relation of the discipline to values and value judgments.

This recognition resulted in at least four distinguishable viewpoints, though they overlapped in the specific statements appearing in the journals and elsewhere. First, some humanitarian-minded sociologists contended that, since the Depression revealed a failure of human rather than technological factors, sociologists had a special responsibility to make their knowledge available and useful in social rehabilitation. Robert S. Lynd's widely read *Knowledge for What?* (1939) proclaims this position. Second, others argued that the socially-conditioned character of values justified research into their origins, cultural variability, and mutual interactions. Proponents of this view insisted that such studies could be pursued without violating objectivity. A third argument declared that the attempt to be "value-free" in order to preserve scientific objectivity is unrealistic, if not impossible. As creatures of their culture, sociologists cannot escape altogether its biases and values (some of which are the values upon which modern science rests). Indeed, the very formulation of a problem in social science implies some kind of evaluation. Therefore objectivity can be achieved more adequately, it was claimed, if the researcher becomes conscious of and explicitly specifies his values. His conclusions can then be judged accordingly. This position was presented clearly and convincingly by Gunnar Myrdal in the Appendices of *An American Dilemma*. Finally, scientific method and scientific knowledge were said to be effective means for attaining any end; science, including sociology, can be used to achieve humanitarian, democratic, manipulative, exploitative, or totalitarian ends. Determining how science will be used is not part of the scientific role of the sociologist, though in his role as a citizen he may legitimately be concerned with the application of science. George A. Lundberg has been a vigorous protagonist of this position.

From the discussion of the relation of values and sociology, as stimulated by the participation of sociologists in government and other organizations oriented toward practical ends, has come a new intellectual justi-fication of sociology. Although the arguments about the relationship of sociology and values sometimes stand in direct opposition, they ulti-mately share a fundamental utilitarianism.

## A New Function for Sociological Theory

As sociologists came to justify their research on more utilitarian grounds and became more aware of the part values play in prompting scientific inquiry their conceptions of the relationship of theory and research changed significantly. Earlier theory had been so intimately linked with the doctrine of progress, social evolution, and philosophies of history, that many sociologists of the second period were inclined to consider theory as an expression of personal bias and value judgements and, therefore, as inimical to the objectivity required in science. But the painstakingly descriptive data collected in the 1920s proved to be inade-quate to meet the demands of the Depression crisis. Recognizing this predicament, many sociologists reconsidered their orientation and at-tempted to make sociology more useful by employing theory or theories to organize and to interrelate the mass of discrete studies. Moreover, some sociologists welcomed this more favorable attitude toward theory, especially the increasing acceptance of the logical systems used to order, articulate, and accumulate research, as a major advance in scientific sociology. Two movements in the late 1930s attest this changing view-point. The one sought to integrate existing sociological concepts, and the other to construct systematic theoretical systems. Both the intellectual traditions of *positivism* and of *social action* (not to be confused with orga-nized action for purposes of social reform) were used to build systematic theories. In recent years social action theory has become particularly prominent.

Theory construction thus appropriately became a scientific guide in the social engineering required by the national crises. Since sociologists argue that "facts do not speak for themselves" but require interpretation, they now generally regard the construction of theory or of conceptual models as indispensable to human engineering projects. In this utilitar-ian era, therefore, "sound theory becomes essentially the most practical thing in the whole scientific realm."[1]

At the same time that systematic theory became a more conspicuous topic in American sociological literature, numerous translations of for-eign theoretical treatises were published. According to the writers' enumeration, which sought to be exhaustive, only twelve books in general theory were published between 1915 and 1935, whereas twenty-seven appeared between 1936 and 1953. Similarly, only six translations of foreign theoretical works appeared between 1915 and 1935, whereas from 1936 to 1953 thirteen such books were published. Theories of Continental scholars were thus more readily available to American sociologists.

The Continental impact on American sociological theory was aided, moreover, by the European political upheavals during the 1930s and 1940s. Forced to emigrate, many scholars came to the United States and joined American academic institutions. Having been trained in the Continental traditions of system-building and abstract philosophical thought, they reinforced the theoretical efforts already in progress in the United States.

## European Influences

Recent European influences on American theory are consequently very pronounced. Among a number of works,* those of the following four theorists are especially significant for American sociology: Vilfredo Pareto (1848–1923), an Italian economist; Emile Durkheim (1858–1917), a French sociologist; Sigmund Freud (1856–1934), an Austrian psychiatrist and founder of psychoanalysis; and Max Weber (1864–1920), a German historian, political economist, and sociologist.

## Pareto

In American intellectual circles of the 1930s Pareto's sociological writings aroused frequent comment. Their importance for American sociological theory rests primarily on Pareto's conception of the *social system*, his tenet that such a system is in equilibrium, his emphasis on the role of non-rationality in human behavior, and his theory of the circulation of the elite.[2]

In order to make sociology a science in spite of the peculiarly variable nature of social phenomena Pareto recommends the *logico-experimental* method as an appropriate investigative procedure. This method embodies two major prerequisites of science: use of logical reasoning and observation of fact without evaluative bias. By applying this procedure to

---

* For example, the writings of Georg Simmel and Karl Mannheim, as well as those of Karl Marx. These have been influential to some small extent in this country, but much less so than the views of Pareto, Durkheim, Freud, and Weber.

a study of society, Pareto believes that it is possible to determine universal, stable social factors and to formulate them as theoretical concepts. Since Pareto assumes that these stable social elements are in mutual dependency, he conceives society as a social system in a state of equilibrium which tends to be reestablished in spite of modifications (induced by internal or external events) producing temporary or permanent change. The concepts for describing society are themselves part of a logically closed system of interrelated and interdependent variables.

These concepts, reflecting the nature of society, ultimately depend on the character of the actions of the component individuals. Pareto maintains that individuals' actions are for the most part nonlogical; they are not based on rational considerations of means and ends. The determining and constant elements in nonlogical behavior are *residues*, or manifestations of sentiments, which are not expressed directly but only indirectly in terms of widely varying *derivations*. * Pareto sets forth a detained classification of both the underlying forces in human conduct — the residues — and the rationalizations or cultural forms in terms of which they are expressed — the derivations. He utilizes his concepts of residues and derivations to explain social classes, social institutions, professional groups, and other social phenomena.

His theory of the circulation of the elite posits that the social classes of the society possess the different residues in varying proportions. Thus the governing elite is always strongly motivated by the residues of "combination" and of the "persistence of aggregates." Yet its position of dominance is secure only so long as it remains willing to use physical force in addition to its manipulation of the masses by appeals to their sentiments and residues. Once the elite loses its ability or willingness to use force, and sometimes also its superior innovating ability, it is overthrown by new leaders. These new rulers who arise from the masses attain powerful positions in society because they do not hesitate to use physical force to attain their ends. That this cycle of change occurs frequently is amply evidenced in the pages of history, for "history is a graveyard of aristocracies."

---

* There are six classes of *residues*: I. residues of combination which account for the combining of ideas and things; II. residues of the persistence of aggregates which account for the adherence to tradition; III. residues of the manifestations of sentiments through overt acts; IV. residues in regard to sociability which make for social conformity; V. residues of the integrity of the individual which make man resist social changes in which he is ego-involved; and VI. sexual residues.

There are four classes of *derivations*: I. affirmations which are statements not based on experience; II. references to authorities which may or may not be empirically sound; III. accord with sentiment or principles, or reference to general consensus; and IV. verbal proofs.

## Durkheim

Though his books were read by numerous American sociologists for many years, Durkheim's ideas were accorded only limited acceptance primarily because they are inconsistent with certain fundamental assumptions of American sociology.[3] The data of sociology, insists Durkheim, are social facts which must be studied as "things" external to and constraining upon the individual. Explanations of social facts belong to lower evolutionary orders such as psychology or biology. Indeed, society itself is a social fact, an entity *sui generis*, something real in itself and unlike a mere sum of the individuals of which it is composed. But most American sociologists have been unwilling to accept this Durkheimian tenet of society as separate and real in itself because their characteristic voluntaristic nominalism has led them to consider society as the sum of individuals in interaction.

Nevertheless, Durkheim's views on social change, his concept of *anomie* (or normlessness), his theory of the categories of thought, and his sociology of religion have become influential. Reflecting the intellectual tenor of his time, Durkheim cast his theories in the context of social evolution. He maintained that societies typically change from a primitive, homogeneous social life marked by *mechanical solidarity* — a unity based on community of ideas, sentiments, and tradition — to industrial, civilized existence with a highly differentiated division of labor, extensive personality variation, and a predominance of contractual relations characterized by *organic solidarity* — a unity based on functional interdependence and sacredness of the individual. Although it undergoes modifications, social solidarity is always the source of social order because it corresponds to the institutionalized norms which constrain individual behavior.

The process of change tends to develop situations in which the old norms no longer restrain individual behavior, and new norms are either absent or unacceptable. Such *anomie*, or normlessness, frequently occurs in the development of urban society, giving rise to personal disorganization and a specific type of suicide which Durkheim calls *anomic suicide*.[4]

Although Durkheim's theory of the categories of thought is formulated as a critique of the nonempirical, a priori mental categories proposed by Immanuel Kant, it is generally interpreted by American sociologists as a contribution to the sociology of knowledge. According to Durkheim, these categories are not innately given. They are developed through human association prevailing at various evolutionary stages of social existence. Such concepts as time, space, force, cause, number, and contradiction are called *collective representations* since they result from the interactions of group life. In the course of evolution the categories accumulate and become permanent parts of the cultural tradition even though the originating conditions may not persist.

Durkheim presented a similarly evolutionary explanation of religious life. Largely on the basis of a case study of the Arunta in Australia, he ascribes the evolutionary origins of religious thought and practice to group existence itself. Thus the major function of religion is the maintenance of social solidarity. In all societies the outstanding characteristic of religion is its distinction between the *sacred* and the *profane*. Things sacred are regarded with awe and reverence and are categorically separate from the commonplace, mundane, or profane.

### Freud

Throughout most of its development American sociology has accepted some and rejected other aspects of Freud's psychological theories.[5] Although psychoanalysis developed primarily as a medical therapy, it influenced American sociology because it recognizes the essential irrationality of human behavior and posits a deterministic theory of personality development.[6] Recently, systematic sociological theorists have employed Freud's concept of the *superego* to construct a logical link between individual motivation and social prescriptions of behavior.[7]

Originally Freud considered behavior as the result of a dialectic process between *Eros*, which is the instinct to live and be active, manifested as the *libido*, and *Thanatos*, which is the death instinct or wish to return to a lifeless state of inactivity. Subsequently, however, Freud placed less emphasis on the death instinct and explained behavior by the interactions within the tripartite structure of human psyche. Specifically, the human psyche is a strictly determined mechanism comprised of the *id*, which is an unconscious force seeking sexual satisfaction in accordance with the "pleasure principle"; the *ego,* which emerges from the id and more or less consciously provides satisfactions in conformity with the "reality principle"; and the *superego*, which evolves from the ego, assimilates the moral standards of the society, and becomes an unconscious conscience. As these psychic components develop during the first five years of life their mutual interaction sets the basic framework of personality. Normal personalities then pass through a latency period from the age of five to thirteen and a pubertal period from the age of thirteen to nineteen, before attaining adulthood. As the personality evolves it maintains an equilibrium among the conflicting id, ego, and superego by the operation of numerous behavior mechanisms. The ones best known and most often utilized by sociologists are repression, sublimation, rationalization, displacement, identification, and projection. Although many other concepts and theories of Freudian psychology are significant contributions to knowledge, their influence on American sociology is less pronounced than these views on motivation and personality development.

## Weber

Of all the modern European intellectuals whose theories are studied by American sociologists, Weber apparently has exerted the dominant influence in recent years.[8] His conceptions of social action and methodology are his most fundamental contributions, though his accomplishments in economics, political science, social history, and comparative religion also impressed American sociologists.

Weber analyzes human conduct as *social action*. Thus all forms of group activity or organization are viewed as ultimately comprised of the actions of individuals whose objective intentions orient their behavior toward the expectations of other persons. It is the task of sociology to explain social action through the special method of understanding (*Verstehen*), which permits interpretation of the subjective motivations of individual actors.

Assuming that such other-oriented individual conduct is dictated, in the ideal case, by rational appraisal of the situation for efficient realization of one's purpose, Weber set forth a classification of social action. Any concrete conduct may be identified with one or a combination of four ideal types of social action, two of which are of maximum rationality. *Purposive* or *expedient action* implies a choice of means calculated to achieve an end with greatest efficiency. However, such a goal is only one of several alternatives in social life and will be pursued only so long as excessive cost in sacrificing other ends is not required. *Value-prescribed action* delimits the choice of possible means in accordance with a single absolute end or value which is pursued irrespective of consequences. The two remaining types of action refer to behavior which is nonrational or irrational rather than primarily rational. Thus, *traditional action* requires the selection of means in keeping with the sanctity of the past (which tends to elevate means to the status of ends). In *emotional* or *affective action* means and ends are linked together in the expression of the actor's emotions or feeling-states. Whenever any type of social action involving two or more actors indicates a set of mutually oriented, subjectively intended expectations, a *social relationship* exists. Weber's fundamentally volitional, individualistic conception of social phenomena is extremely congenial to voluntaristic nominalism and thus makes his theory particularly attractive to American sociologists.

Weber's methodological arguments arrested the attention of several American sociologists during the development of systematic theory in the late 1930s. The subsequent dissemination and frequent acceptance of his methodological principles suggest their congeniality with much of American sociology. They are not only consistent with individualism generally, but are designed to make the social sciences as precise and certain as the natural sciences without relinquishing the distinctions between them. Accepting the traditional German contrast between the *Geisteswissenschaften* (social sciences) and the *Naturwissenschaften* (natural sciences), Weber argues that the precision attained in the natural sciences by strict mathematical methods can also be achieved in the social sciences by the use of logical analysis and procedure.

Furthermore, Weber denies that the natural sciences alone have a monopoly on generalized theoretical categories. This conviction, coupled with his emphasis on logic, led him to develop the methodological principle of *ideal types* for use in the social realm. Since social phenomena can be viewed from many perspectives, depending particularly upon the values involved in the situation and the original problem formulated by the investigator, they must be precisely conceptualized by the sociologist in order that systematic comparison with other social phenomena can be undertaken. An ideal type is thus a specifically defined, meaningful constellation which is genetic in nature (because it must contain the motives of action) and is a deliberate intensification and overemphasis of certain aspects of concrete events (because it is viewed from one selected perspective).

In his own writings Weber employs two major kinds of ideal types. On the one hand, he develops concepts of unique historical individuals or events, for example, modern capitalism which is characterized by the religious ethic of Protestantism. On the other hand, he isolates recurrent factors or common conditions such as rational-legal, traditional, and charismatic types of authority, which are present in various social institutions or historical events.

Weber himself demonstrates the applicability of his methodological principles by extensive historical investigations. He studied the bureaucratic mode of social organization in Modern Western society, analyzed social stratification, and compared the great world religions of Hinduism, Confucianism, and Christianity. Recently these empirical researches have also exercised considerable influence on American sociologists.

It may be surprising that the writings of Karl Marx, which stimulated Weber and many other European intellectuals, exercised relatively little influence on American sociology. Marx's explanations of class structure and its relation to social change, political institutions, the family, ideologies, science, and religion stimulated some sociologists in this country to examine these same topics, but usually led them to different conclusions. The basic reason for the nonacceptance of Marxist theories appears to derive from his economic determinism, which is often interpreted as a fundamental denial of American individualism and which is inconsistent with the multicausational position of most American sociologists.

In sum, the national emergencies of the third era in American sociology not only encouraged the application of scientific knowledge in the resolution of practical problems, but also contributed to the emergence of a new function for sociological theory. The resulting development of theory owes many of its ideas and basic principles to the sociological works of European scholars, especially Pareto, Durkheim, Freud, and Weber. Although some of the conceptions of these four men are incompatible with the problems, assumptions, and interests of modern American sociologists, others are very congenial, particularly those pertaining to the motivation of action, the interrelatedness of social wholes, the process of change, and scientific methodology. The significance of these timely contributions of European theorists is evident in the recent attempts at systematic theory construction based on the traditions of positivism or social action which are examined in the following pages.

## Sociological Neo-Positivism: Lundberg

The leading exponent of neo-positivism in contemporary American sociology is George A. Lundberg. After receiving his M.A. and Ph.D. degrees at the universities of Wisconsin and Minnesota, respectively, he embarked on a teaching and research career which carried him across the United States. He was a member of the faculties of the University of Pittsburgh, Columbia University, and Bennington College in the East. In 1945 he returned to the University of Washington (where he held his first academic appointment) to become Walker Ames Professor and head of the Department of Sociology.

Although Lundberg insists that sociologists must scrupulously separate their roles as scientists and citizens, he justifies sociology as a science on the grounds of its practical utility for obtaining social objectives. (But he avoids the question of *whose* objectives sociology should serve.) Like Comte, his positivistic predecessor, he views social disorganization as a consequence of the coexistence within society of inconsistent principles of knowledge — the theological, metaphysical, and scientific. Our social order might be reorganized and stabilized, he contends, on the basis of any one of these principles. However, the prevalent technologically-induced interdependence of our civilization, based largely on science, demands that scientific or positivistic principles be used. Sociology's ultimate instrumental function is to aid in this scientific reorganization of society.

As the science of human relations, sociology "can save us," though it cannot prescribe the ends men should seek or how the knowledge of the various sciences (including sociology) should be used.[9] But Lundberg is convinced that our common humanity confers general agreement on these ends and that conflict arises "over the means toward these ends, as represented by fantastic ideologies." Sociology's practical contribution is first, to formulate possible alternatives of action under given conditions and second, to indicate the means, expense, and near and remote consequences of alternative social policies. By demonstrating its ability to predict these consequences and to calculate the achievability, the costs, and the compatibility of men's aspirations, sociology can itself condition men's choices. The determination of probable effects of different social programs and policies requires knowledge of the "natural" laws of human behavior which are not limited to the conditions of specific cultures but possess the same universality as the laws of gravity. If men wish to achieve organization and peace, they must abide by the restrictions that these fundamental laws of conduct impose.

For sociology to provide reliable predictions it must reappraise its assumptions, concepts, techniques, and methodology in the light of the demands of natural science.[10] Lundberg concludes that mathematics, social measuring instruments, "operational definitions," a consistent frame of reference, and a logically coherent, empirically verifiable system of concepts are indispensable for the discovery of predictive sociological generalizations and laws.

These generalizations must involve enumeration, Lundberg argues, for they are statements of the probable prevalence of a social phenomenon or a configuration of social data. To attain maximum predictive value, generalizations must be stated mathematically. When these statements indicating the statistical probability of the occurrence of an event under specified conditions have been empirically verified, they become laws. Reliable, verifiable observations on which such generalizations are based require such standardized measuring instruments as attitude scales, opinion thermometers, and the like. Through instruments of this kind concepts may be defined in terms of the operations by which data are obtained, that is, "operationally." "Intelligence," for example, is *that which* intelligence tests measure or, in a different area, "opinion" is *that which* polling techniques provide. Lundberg claims that if concepts are to be standardized, communicable, and useful for science, this operational procedure is essential.

The content of concepts reflects the basic assumptions, axioms, and postulates of any discipline. As the frame of reference for sociology, these presuppositions should be rigorously examined to see if they meet the demands of natural science. Using arguments drawn from Pareto, Lundberg insists that this frame of reference must be organized so as to constitute the basis for a logically consistent and coherent abstract conceptual system.[11] The system of basic concepts should be applicable to all concrete situations, events, or behavior which sociology investigates. Through their combinations and permutations, these concepts furnish the basis for hypotheses and permit their systematic testing. Study along these lines provides the only adequate source of predictive generalizations in sociology.

The content of the frame of reference which Lundberg tries to establish for sociology is calculated to make the discipline a genuine *social physics* (to use Comte's term). Lundberg defines sociology as the study of inter-human activity, including intrahuman or "inner" behavior which has other people as a point of reference. This definition resembles the basic postulate of the social action frame of reference, to be considered shortly. However, Lundberg regards inter-human activity as a system of energy within a field of force, changes in which are fundamentally forms of energy transformation within the physical cosmos — like changes in other aspects of the universe. Observable social behavior is viewed as the consequence of energy-determining attractions or repulsions and similarities or dissimilarities (such as status, age, sex, beliefs, and economic positions) operating within a field of force. Included in this field are the behavior in question and the total environment — a situation to be investigated as a "closed system."

Lundberg's social-physical (or natural science) conception of human society represents an adaptation of the theories of Frederic Le Play and Patrick Geddes, although it had been worked out independently by Stuart Dodd, now Lundberg's colleague. Without attempting to introduce Dodd's detailed mathematical symbolism, Lundberg agrees with the latter that any social situation can be described in terms of the formula: "(S)ocial situation equals (P)opulations with certain (I)ndicators of characteristics changing in (T)ime and/or spatial (L)ength"; or $S = P:I:T:L$. Population may be classified as social categories and types of groups. Indicators involve the basic social process of communication (expressed in association and dissociation), institutions and demographic variations. The time variable, or societal change, involves processes and factors of change such as invention. The spatial variable, or (L)ength, includes factors and processes of human ecology. In their various possible combinations these four fundamental, generalized conceptual variables $(P, I, T, L)$ should serve to describe any social situation or form of interhuman activity. More specialized concepts, their operational definitions, construction of measuring devices, and the derivation of hypotheses for empirical verification in research should use as their starting point these four basic concepts of the natural science system of human society.

Lundberg's continuing endeavor to develop a sociology modeled upon the physical sciences, especially physics, has had considerable influence among younger sociologists. His emphasis on the use of statistical procedures is in keeping with efforts to conduct sociological research more rigorously and with greater precision. But the implications of behaviorism and so-called physicalism in his position still seem to contradict the pervasive voluntarism of American sociology. Appropriately, a vigorous opposition has come from the exponents of the social action theory which is now to be surveyed. (Moreover, it is legitimate to regard the disagreement between the neo-positivist Lundberg and the social action theorists as a continuation of the subjectivism-objectivism controversy of the late

1920s and the early 1930s. MacIver, who is currently associated with the social action viewpoint, defended the position of subjectivism while Lundberg was a protagonist of objectivism and statistics.)[12]

## Social Action Theory

Since World War II social action theory (as noted earlier, not to be confused with social reform efforts) has become the dominant theoretical perspective in American sociology. In addition to the obvious advantage of having its principal proponents strategically located in leading university centers, this orientation owes its ascendance, at least in part, to its adoption and further development of a unified, logically consistent and integrated system and, it may be argued, to its commitment to an essentially voluntaristic, individualistic interpretation of social behavior traditional in American sociology (which neo-positivism, by its association with behaviorism, seems to threaten or question).

Four sociologists — Florian Znaniecki, Robert M. MacIver, Howard P. Becker, and Talcott Parsons — have been primarily responsible for the development of social action theory in this country, though its intellectual antecedents go back ultimately to German idealist social science traditions and, more immediately, to Max Weber in particular. Of the four, Becker and Parsons have most explicitly credited Weber as inspiring their theoretical formulations. But whether directly influenced or not, all four scholars are in fundamental agreement with Weber's conception of social action as conduct guided by awareness of other persons whose behavior is regarded by the actor as affecting attainment of his own needs. From this postulate various implications have been deduced, which together constitute what has come to be termed the *action frame of reference.*

The first proposition of this frame of reference or set of assumptions, in which Znaniecki, MacIver, Becker, and Parsons concur, holds that group behavior must be referred back to, and becomes meaningful in terms of the subjective intentions of the individual participants. Conduct toward others is impelled by motives.* It aims at the attainment of purposes, ends, or goals. Social action involves the satisfaction of wishes, attitudes, or dispositions in the form of values and interests. It seeks,

---

* All of the theorists under consideration are interested in the study of motives in relation to social control and cultural prescriptions. MacIver specifically regards the investigation of individual motives (as distinct from social pressures or sanctions) as a psychological task not within the province of sociology.

argues Parsons, to optimize gratification and minimize deprivations. Other-directed activity is thus individually *teleological* in nature.

A second proposition of the action frame of reference states that goal-oriented conduct occurs in a situation, at a specific place and time. Aspects of the situation which are unchangeable are *conditions* with which any actor must reckon, whereas the aspects which can be changed and manipulated by the actor in attaining his goals are the *means*.

A third proposition in this set of assumptions, to which only Becker seems to express clear dissent, maintains that there are always alternative means to ends or alternative ends themselves which require exercise of choice. This view finds its expression in the recurrent use of the terms *selection, evaluation, judgment,* and (dynamic) *assessment*. However, choice in human conduct is neither wholly random nor entirely circumscribed by conditions: it tends to be limited by social codes, cultural standards, and institutional norms.

Although other propositions about social conduct may be deduced from the definition given above, the minimal components of the action frame of reference are means, ends, conditions, and norms. Parsons, in fact, views them as comprising the terms of the unit act — the fundamental datum of sociological study.

The social action approach also implies that sociologists should study material that symbolizes or expresses the subjective intentions of actors. Thus Znaniecki, MacIver, Becker, and Parsons agree that information drawn from the actor's own testimony is of basic importance in analyzing the determinants of conduct. According to Znaniecki and MacIver, the sociologist is justified in using data from the person's own experience because the individual is aware of himself and others as conscious personalities (that is, he is characterized by what Znaniecki calls the "humanistic coefficient"). MacIver's view that the individual's own testimony should be invoked to aid in the "sympathetic reconstruction" of the factors involved in behavior is consistent with his insistence that consciousness or awareness is an intrinsic aspect of social relationships (as distinct from nonsocial relationships of the type studied in the physical sciences).

In short, Znaniecki, MacIver, Becker, and Parsons concur in their basic views on social action. They accept Weber's conception of social action. They agree that means, ends, conditions, and institutional norms are basic components of the social action system. And all of them urge the use of data drawn from the actor's own perspective and experience as indispensable to fruitful analysis of social behavior. Since social action as a logical system has been elaborated in different directions, the particular contributions of each theorist must now be examined.

## Znaniecki

Although Florian Znaniecki's uninterrupted participation in American sociological circles began only in 1939, his work had been known for some time through his publications, especially *The Polish Peasant in Europe and America* (1918–1920), of which he was co-author with W. I. Thomas, and his teaching as a visiting professor at the University of Chicago and Columbia University. Until World War II he had been a member of the faculty of the University of Poznan in Poland, the country in which he was born and received his training in philosophy and sociology. In 1940 he joined the Sociology Department of the University of Illinois, where he taught until his recent retirement. His major fields of sociological study are methodology, sociology of knowledge, nationalism, the nature and history of social thought, and sociological theory.[13]

Znaniecki's *Social Actions* (1936) and *Cultural Sciences* (1952) are especially devoted to the analysis of the structure and processes of social action. In any social situation, Znaniecki observes, the individual or agent tries to affect the behavior of a *social object*, the primary human target who is crucial to the agent's purposes. The agent attempts to influence the social object by using certain *social instruments* (or mechanisms at his disposal in the situation) in a certain fashion called the *social method*. The modification of the activities of the object as they appear to the agent is termed the *social reaction*. To a salesman, for example, the potential customer is a social object. The desired reaction, sale of an article, may be secured by the method of persuasively flattering the customer. Advertising, price lists, even the product itself may be used as instruments to effect a sale.

Any particular action is based on the subject's or agent's conception of the possibilities to be actualized or prevented in the situation in accordance with his purposes. This *definition of the situation* depends on his own attitudes and on relevant *standards of value* and *norms of conduct*. The agent thus normally believes that there are certain standards by which people and things in the situation should be valued and certain norms according to which people ought to act in the situation. When he and others in the situation behave in conformity with these standards and norms, their actions are patterned. Znaniecki calls such ordered actions *axionormative*, for both standards of value and norms have been applied to the conduct.

Nonconformist behavior results when persons' actions deviate further from the ideals than the permissible variation. These transgressions of recognized standards and values are causes of *cultural disorganization* which, in turn, requires *cultural reorganization*. Members of action systems ordinarily try to counteract violations by various forms of repression, such as banishment and imprisonment. Often the participation of representatives or members of an action system in punishing transgressors serves to strengthen the solidarity and accentuate the conformity of the group. This effect is termed a *conservative reorganization* of the action system. For example, the fact that the Spanish branch of the Roman Catholic Church is more conservative and stricter in its conformity than other branches of the Church may be the consequences of its conflict with Islam, the expulsion of the Jews and Moors, and its active opposition to Protestantism. An action system may undergo *creative reorganization*, a second type, by the gradual introduction of new values, cultural patterns of action, or new relationships of functional interdependence. Cooperation comes to replace former conflict within or between action systems.

These ordered (organized) and disordered (disorganized) actions involve various processes which are dependent on the actor's appraisal of the social object's attitudes toward the actor's own purposes. Those actions arising from a favorable evaluation of the social object's attitudes toward the subject's ends are classified as forms of accommodation, for they require some mutual adjustment of activities and attitudes. (This process is further subdivided on the basis of whether or not the person shows initiative or passivity in evoking the object's positive reactions.) If the person in question believes that the object is negatively disposed toward the attainment of his ends, his action is a form of opposition, either defensive or aggressive. When the individual acts positively because he is favorably inclined toward the object for the object's own sake, the action is a type of altruism. To act only for the sake of harming the object is a form of hostility.

Znaniecki's basic methodology and conception of social causation most closely resemble the views of Robert M. MacIver, a personal friend and colleague during Znaniecki's lectureship at Columbia University. In view of their intellectual similarity, it is now appropriate to consider MacIver's contribution to social action theory.

## MacIver

Like Znaniecki, MacIver is not a native American sociologist. He was born in Scotland where he also acquired his intellectual training and early academic experience. After receiving his doctorate at the University of Edinburgh, he taught at the University of Aberdeen. Later he went to Canada to join the University of Toronto faculty and from there he came to Columbia University in 1927. During his more than twenty years of academic life at Columbia he was especially active in studying political sociology, intergroup relations, and social action theory.[14] His principal contributions to action theory include a methodological theory, classification of social structures, a typology of societies, and interpretations of social change and social causation.

MacIver's social action theory is ultimately based on his conception of social relationships. As the field of study for sociology, social relationships differ from physical and organic relationships in being determined by the mutual recognition of beings endowed with consciousness. Since mutual recognition requires that individuals be subjectively aware of other persons as objects, MacIver's conception of social relationships necessarily involves the subject-object distinction of social action theory. To use MacIver's own terms, both "attitudes," or subjective dispositions toward objects, and "interests," or objects toward which attitudes are directed, are involved in social behavior. Attitudes are primarily associative and dissociative. Interests are like and common. *Like interests* are enjoyed or pursued distributively or separately by each individual privately, whereas *common interests* must be sought collectively and shared without division. The like interest may be illustrated by the credits toward which college students work. But the college life in which they participate is shared. Of course, the like may also become the basis for common interest. In addition, common interests are divided into two types which are particularly relevant to the analysis of social relationships. The first entails identification of men with some inclusive, indivisible social unity, such as in-group loyalty to an ethnic group. The second type involves attachment to some impersonal goal or endeavor, for example, the furtherance of the prohibitionist cause. MacIver's general concept of common interest further emphasizes the fundamental subject-object difference between attitudes and interests. Attitudes may be harmonious, but they cannot be common, for the subjective element is always individualized and private. But people can have common interests, just as they have common possessions.

Since the individual experiences groups as objects to be used in attaining ends or as constraints on his conduct, MacIver's concept of interest is the point of departure for classifying social groups into three principal varieties. The first general type involves inclusive social groupings which occupy a limited territory and are characterized by unspecialized interests. Community, the generic type, is an unplanned inclusive network of relationships arising from the sharing of the basic conditions of common living on a common soil. The second general type includes social groupings conscious of general interests which have not, however, crystallized into permanent and definite organizations. Class, ethnic, and racial groups, and crowds are generic types. Social groupings with specific interests and specific and enduring organizations constitute the third general type. These groups are organized purposefully to attain a distinct interest. The generic type is the association, with the primary group, and large-scale association as the two subtypes. Using interest as a criterion, these two subvarieties are further divided into primary and secondary forms. Primary interests, which are the basis for primary groups, are cultural in nature and are pursued for their own sake, for direct satisfaction. Secondary interests, which are the basis for large-scale associations, are utilitarian and civilizational in nature and are desired because they are *means* to satisfactions. Large-scale associations are further classified as economic, political, and technological.

Implicit in the typology just outlined is an evolutionary formulation of social change. In its earlier phases society as a social structure was *communal*. More recently, society has become *associational*, with groups of the third general type conspicuous in its organization. This change is evolutionary in that increasing differentiation (and integration) are entailed.*

Communal or primitive society is characterized by "primitive fusion." Utilitarian means and cultural ends are integrated. The instruments of making a living are pervasively intertwined with customs and tradition. The society is an inclusive community by blood or kinship and by occupation of a common territory. Membership in the few social groupings, based on kinship, age, or sex criteria, is obligatory. Age and sex differences are the primary bases for division of labor. Large-scale voluntary associations do not exist.

Later, certain social functions tend to become vested in particular

---

* Division of labor has increased so that specializations and functional interdependence have become more intricate. Each of the functional associations and institutions, which become more numerous and varied, is specific and limited in its range of services. And, finally, the instruments of communication have become more diverse and refined.

subgroups in the society. The rights and privileges attached to such functions as religious or magical activities come to be distinguished from the general, customary codes. Thus specific modes of procedures, or new *institutions*, are formed. MacIver terms this intermediate phase the *stage of differentiated communal institutions.*

Associational, or modern, civilized society is socially differentiated. Means and ends are separated into two distinctive realms, and primitive fusion has been destroyed. Culture itself is no longer bound to the land or to the kinship groups. The now elaborate division of labor is an intricate functional interdependence. The emergence of large-scale associations, voluntarily organized in accordance with specialized interests, implies the accomplishment of the intellectually difficult feat of combining likenesses and differences. Since society no longer integrates values for the individual, choice must be exercised. Society itself is characterized by a unity which is multiform rather than uniform.

For MacIver the process of social change as well as social causation itself depends on the operation of *dynamic assessment.* Social change is initiated by the changing choices or judgments of interrelated individuals who interpret, evaluate, or assess situations. Any one or more of four factors which impinge on the choices in and appraisals of the situation may lead to social change. Alteration in the cultural system of values governing the selection of goals or aims; in the society's utilitarian devices and techniques providing means for ends; in the social relations acting as an agency, obstacle, or goal of action; and in the physical-organic conditions relevant to and necessary for attaining a goal — all are sources of change. But these factors are dynamic only as they are subjectively apprehended and assessed and brought into a coherent and consistent unity by individuals and groups.

MacIver is one of the two exponents of social action who are fundamentally preoccupied with the problem of social change. Howard Becker, the other, has made the explanation of social change the central concern of his analytic scheme.

## Becker

Howard Becker is the only social action theorist who is American both by birth and by academic training. He was a student of the late Professor Robert E. Park at the University of Chicago, where he received his Ph.D. Since 1937 he has been a professor of sociology at the University of Wisconsin. Throughout his career he has been especially preoccupied with the history of social thought and the development of sociological theory.[15] His persistent interest in the problem of social change is illustrated by his researches on German peasant villages and the mentality of the ancient Greeks, among other writings.

Apart from the constructed type methodology, Becker's principal theoretical contribution consists of his application of social action theory to the study of social change. His action theory makes use of G. H. Mead's interpretation of the significance of symbols, Max Weber's types of relations between means and ends, Znaniecki's differentiation of the components of an action situation, and W. I. Thomas' four wishes.

According to Becker, the specific values of the larger society are the context for social action in any concrete situation. These values are a context because they have become interwoven in the personality of the course of past socialization. Needs of any normally socialized person are both culturally and interpersonally defined by the shared cultural values. Learning the culture requires the acquisition of symbols which, in turn, is possible only by direct personal interaction and role-playing. Accordingly, the socialized individual's needs are necessarily defined and satisfied through ends or purposes oriented to others and through values shared with others by communication. By a transformation of Thomas' scheme of the four wishes, Becker classifies the final ends of action as new experience, response, recognition, and security. Both needs and ends of social action are related to values by use of Mead's interpretation of the role of the symbol. Since social action is value-defined action, its analysis — contends Becker — entails study of the impact of the society's value system on the concrete circumstances of action.

To interpret the specific course of goal-oriented action in a given situation, Becker employs analytic distinctions earlier devised by Znaniecki and Weber. In accordance with Znaniecki's analysis of the action situation, Becker notes that any actor will be oriented toward a social object or person and will select a particular method and an instrument or instruments to try to evoke a desired response from the social object. Becker also uses Weber's means-ends typology to classify the possible relationships between means (Znaniecki's method and instruments) and ends (the purposes of the actor). If a person's choice of means to attain a certain end is governed only by considerations of minimizing effort and undesirable consequences and maximizing efficiency, the means-ends relationship is termed *expedient rationality*. "Cold-blooded calculation" is its hallmark. When the end itself limits or prescribes the kinds of means which can be used (over and beyond mere efficiency), the means-ends relationship is called *sanctioned rationality*. For example, the Christian ethic forbids the use of force in making one love one's neighbor as one's self. In the third type, *traditional nonrationality*, what were once means are elevated to the rank of ends. The role of the fasces in recent times as contrasted with its role in Roman military discipline is illustrative. The *fasces*, an axe with a number of rods lashed about it, is now a commonly employed emblem of unchanging justice, whereas it was once used to discipline Roman soldiers. *Affective nonrationality*, the fourth type, represents a fairly complete fusion of means and ends when it is incorporated as a chief phase of an action. It includes everything from outbursts of love or hatred to the unquestioning, emotionalized acceptance of a leader.

All of these conceptual distinctions — personal needs, cultural values, means, ends, means-ends relationships — are utilized in Becker's analysis of social change. For this purpose Becker also amplifies and elaborates the conceptions of sacred and secular societies earlier proposed by Park. As constructed types, the sacred-secular dichotomy can be applied to the investigation of concrete societies. In a sacred society the value systems, social action, and personalities are characterized by a maximum aversion to change, by a tendency to respond negatively, or to reject the new as it is defined in the society. Because the society is spatially, socially, and mentally isolated, its value system is rigid and relatively impermeable. Its members seek the ends of response, recognition, and especially security. The means by which these ends are sought are primarily those of traditional nonrationality and sanctioned rationality. In contrast, the value systems, social action, and personalities of a secular society show a maximum of readiness and capacity to change, to respond positively, or to accept the new as it is defined in the society. Since the society is spatially, socially, and mentally accessible to the stimuli of change, its value systems are flexible and permeable. Recognition, response, and especially new experience are the desired ends of its members, which are attained primarily by the means of expedient rationality and affective nonrationality.

Each of these two types of society is further divided into subtypes. If a sacred society shows a diffuse opposition to change because it is tradition-bound and invokes traditionally nonrational means, it is classified as a folk (or traditional) sacred society. Many preliterate societies, though not all, fall into this subtype. The Alabama and Missouri communities described by H. C. Nixon in *Possum Trot: Rural Community, South* (1941) and by James West in *Plainville, U.S.A.* (1945) also belong in this category. If the antagonism to change becomes organized and specified by a set of rigid, explicit prescriptions and injunctions and if the society tends to use means of the sanctioned rationality variety, it is a prescribed- (or sanctioned) sacred society. A totalitarian kind of structure usually results, such as the Geneva theocracy of Calvin, the Jesuit state of Paraguay, Nazi Germany, Fascist Italy, and Soviet Russia. A secular society which is inclined to favor change consistent with certain flexible, generalized principles and which often tends to use expediently rational means to attain security as the dominant end is principled- (or stable) secular society. The social life of Middle-class urban Americans is suggestive of this variety. When change is welcomed simply because it is new, when experience is the dominant end sought by affectively nonrational means, the society is termed a normless (or unstable) secular society. Modern "emancipated" circles of cosmopolitan urban centers are the closest approximation to this type. Admittedly there is a point beyond which even an extreme secular society cannot go if it is to remain a society. Something sacred must persist — some goals in common, a value system with ends in some respects shared — for a collection of human beings pursuing at random a systemless mass of discrete ends is scarcely a society.

These four major types of societies represent points on a continuum of sacredness and secularity. Any concrete society can thus be examined with reference to its position on this continuum. The impact of particular social changes can be interpreted as producing more or less sacralization or secularization in the society.

Becker's action theory, as well as those of Znaniecki and MacIver, stands in contrast to the social system formulation of Talcott Parsons, the last of the major action theorists whose intellectual position is now to be outlined. Of the four major sociologists, only Parsons explicitly incorporates in his theory implications drawn from Freud and Pareto.

## Parsons

Talcott Parsons, who was born in the United States and received his doctorate in economics from the University of Heidelberg (Germany), is an unusually influential social action theorist. He has contributed well-known analyses of kinship, social stratification, political movements, mass communications, and the professions, especially medicine.[16] But his recent development of a theory of the social system has evoked particularly wide-spread comment in American sociology.[17] In 1946 Parsons became the first chairman of the new interdisciplinary Department of Social Relations at Harvard University where he had been teaching since 1927.

Like Lundberg, Parsons accepts Pareto's view that an abstract system of concepts is required for the scientific study and analysis of social phenomena. But he differs from Lundberg in using the action frame of reference, or set of assumptions about social thought, for deriving the concepts which are the categories or parts of his logically closed system. Combining aspects of the theories of Kant, Weber, and Freud, Parsons proposes that any study of social relations must start with an actor (or subject) who is oriented to a situation composed of physical, cultural, and social objects. The subject's action is prompted by one or a combination of three modes of motivational orientation. The *cognitive mode* involves cognition or an interest in knowing or defining aspects of the situation. The *cathetic mode* indicates cathexis or an interest in securing maximum gratification of needs-dispositions. And the *evaluative mode* refers to evaluation or to interest in ordered choice from the possible objects in the situation.

With this conception of the action frame of reference, Parsons undertakes the analysis of social behavior. He observes that the interaction of two persons is entirely different from the action of a single action oriented to a nonsocial object. Social objects (other persons) can respond and, therefore, can affect the gratification which the particular person is seeking. Hence the action of any individual toward another person must always take into consideration what alternatives are open to the other individual and that his own choices will influence what the other person decides to do. The obverse is true for the other person — the social object. Accordingly, each individual is oriented to the expectations of the other persons in social interaction. Stable interactions require a shared common set of moral standards so that each individual knows what to expect from the other in the situation. When these stable and regulated motivated interactions of two or more actors are oriented toward one another and toward a collective goal so that they constitute an organized system, they are termed a *social system*.

The basic unit of the social system as well as the smallest stable sector of situationally specific interactions is the *role*. Actual overt conduct of an individual as a member of a group in a socially defined situation comprises a role. However, the actor's conduct is guided by a shared moral standard of what he and other individuals believe he ought to do. Ordinarily he is motivated to conform to this role-expectation, for the rule will have been incorporated in his personality during his earlier socialization. He now regards adherence to the expected conduct as the normal way to fulfill his needs. He feels pride in living up to the dictates of his conscience. And, moreover, he wants and needs the social approval which can be secured by conformity. For example, part of the role of a member of a delinquent gang is to refuse to "squeal" on the others if he is caught by the police. He has learned that the way to be a success is to abide by the code. He expects to gain social commendation from other members for conforming to the rule and, conversely, he feels shame if he unwittingly divulges information to the legal authorities. The actual role will tend to coincide with the role expectation if the rule or standard involved has been institutionalized. This process of *institutionalization* has occurred if conformity to the role-expectation has become a way of satisfying the needs of any actor as well as a condition for maximizing the gratifications of other persons in the situation. Thus, Parsons' concept of the role interlocks motivation, gratification, and choice with the prevalence of shared standards and stability.

Furthermore, the social system is comprised of various kinds of roles or constellations of roles which are termed *institutions*. Only through the performance of differentiated roles can the social system operate as a system. The nature of minimum roles is prescribed by the conditions which any self-subsistent social system must meet if it is to persist. These necessary conditions, or *functional prerequisites*, are set by the scarcity of desired objects in any action situation, the nature of the human organism, and the realities of orderly coexistence among the actors in a situation.

Parsons outlines four general types of institutions or constellations of roles which are common to self-subsistent social systems or societies. Based on the subject-object distinction in the frame of reference, *relational* institutions classify and limit the roles which actors may legitimately assume as subjects and as objects (apart from their interest in one another). Parsons subdivides these institutions into orientation roles, or subject roles, and object roles, or roles played as objects of orientation. *Regulative* institutions classify and limit the roles which actors may legitimately assume with reference to goals and means of one another's interests. Claims to objects, either as *facilities* (objects desired for the uses to which they can be put) or as *rewards* (objects desired for their own sake, as direct ends of gratification), must be institutionally regulated if the social system is to persist in equilibrium. Economic and political institutions regulate access to facilities and social stratification regulates access to rewards. *Integrative* institutions fulfil the functional prerequisite of negative and positive co-ordination in the social system. These institutions prevent disruptive interferences among the roles and facilitate the achievement of shared goals through collective action. So-called responsibility roles for both private and public interests are included in this type of institution. *Cultural* institutions are distinctive in that they involve acceptance of value patterns rather than commitments to action. Science, religion, philosophy, and art are classified as cultural institutions. *

Just as motivation to conform is crucial to the ordered performance of roles embodied in these four types of institutions, so deviant motivation is the source of change in the social system. Social change is ultimately a problem of individual deviations which have become so recurrent and focalized that mechanisms of social control are no longer effective. The lack of coincidence of individual gratifications with shared role-expectations is the basic mechanism for explaining the impetus to change, its persistence and extension, and stabilization in the social system.

Parsons' theoretical formulations have had widespread intellectual repercussions in American sociology. His influence has been exercised both through his own publications and those of his students, such as Marion Levy and Wilbert Moore of Princeton University, Robin Williams of Cornell University, and Kingsley Davis and Robert Merton of Columbia University. Though all of these sociologists have made independent contributions, Merton's theory and research have particularly provoked sociological comment and discussion.


## Theories of the Middle Range: Merton

Robert K. Merton, professor of sociology at Columbia University since 1941, has an intellectual orientation both similar to and different from that of Talcott Parsons, his former teacher. Like Parsons, he regards science as an abstract, generalized theoretical system of logically consistent and interdependent assumptions, concepts, and propositions; his theory is also based on the means-ends scheme of social action; and his analytic paradigm, or statement of prescriptions for conducting re-

---

* This usage of the word *culture* is consistent with that of R. M. MacIver.

search, is used in the same way as Parsons employs his elaborate theoretical system.

Merton differs conspicuously from Parsons in his view about the level at which profitable theorization can now occur. He does not agree that sociology should seek an integrated or master conceptual scheme at present. He declares, rather, that the discipline can advance only by devoting major concern to what are known as *theories of the middle range*, that is, those intermediate to routine research hypotheses and an inclusive conceptual system. This level involves special theories applicable to limited ranges of data, for example, theories about social class, bureaucracy, and interpersonal influence.

Although he hardly depreciates theory, Merton seems to be somewhat more acutely sensitive to empirical fact and research in sociological inquiry than is Parsons. Indeed, he insists that theory and research are reciprocally interrelated in science. His formulation of their interrelations has been so favorably received that textbooks in methods of social research are now incorporating it.[18]

Recognizing that any investigation is conducted on the basis of certain assumptions, Merton contends that the researcher's orientation should be made explicit as an analytic paradigm. He urges use of the paradigm to prevent unwitting importation of outside assumptions into the research, to facilitate the codification of methods, and to aid in accumulating theoretical interpretations and in sensitizing the sociologist to related theoretical or empirical problems.

Merton follows Parsons in accepting a functionalist conception of society. His analytic paradigm is also functionalist. But Merton's paradigm does not show the theoretical comprehensiveness or logical elaborateness of Parsons' social system, for Merton is committed to middle-range theories. Accordingly, Merton's paradigm stipulates only the minimum requirements for the functional study of social structure and change. Nevertheless, he describes eleven separate aspects of functional analysis, involving specification of assumptions, concepts, analytic procedures, and methods of validation.[19]

The most crucial of all of these aspects is the identification of function.[20] But an understanding of function is impossible without the knowledge, as the functional theorist conceives it, of society as an operating whole of interrelated and interdependent parts. The components of society act and react on one another and on the entire system. These actions tend to have objective consequences for the organization of a society. An objective consequence of a social or cultural item (such as a role or status) which contributes to the survival, persistence, integration, or stability of the society as a whole is a *function*. If such an effect, however, contributes to the disintegration or instability of the society or any of its segments and lessens its possibility of survival and persistence, it is termed a *dysfunction*. When the positive objective consequences are intended and recognized by persons involved, such effects are called *manifest functions*. If they are unintended and unrecognized, they are termed *latent functions*.

The inclusion of the concept of dysfunction in the paradigm is very important, for it indicates how the study of social change may be approached from a functionalist perspective. The instability characterizing dysfunction suggests stress, strain, tension, and disequilibrium — the social conditions out of which deviation and change may arise in a social system.

Although the concept of dysfunction is not the specific point of departure for Merton's paper "Social Structure and Anomie," it is concretely illustrated in this essay on change and reactions to change. Here Merton is especially concerned with the emergence of deviant forms of role adaptations in a social structure, such as contemporary American society, which places a disproportionate emphasis on the cultural goals as opposed to the institutional rules regulating realization of goals. These deviant forms include *innovation* (the use of institutionally forbidden but effective means of attaining accepted goals), *ritualism* (abandonment of lofty goals accompanied by meticulous adherence to institutional rules), *retreatism* (passive withdrawal from sanctioned cultural goals and institutional means), and *rebellion* (rejection of both prevailing goals and means and the active effort to institute different goals and means).

Merton employs various aspects of the generalized functional paradigm in other studies of modern American society. His inquiries concentrate on certain phases of modern mass organization: bureaucracy, mass communications, and the social consequences of science.[21] Using functional analysis, he interprets two problems of contemporary bureaucratic structure. He suggests how such organizations develop a formalistic, ritualistic adherence to procedure, which is dysfunctional to the point of vitiating the actual purpose of the structure, as well as how strains are evoked in the structure by recruitment of social scientists as bureaucrats.

Merton's concern with the functional interdependence of thought and belief and social structure leads him to define the relations between the two related, though distinct, fields of the sociology of knowledge and the sociology of mass communications. *Mass Persuasion*, which is a study of the Kate Smith marathon radio war-bond drive of September, 1943, exemplifies the use of functional inquiry in mass communications. The war-bond drive is analyzed as an interdependent conjuncture of: (1) the immediate situation (a radio marathon) as a device for riveting the attention of a large audience upon a single person; (2) the content of the appeals (or themes) communicated by that person (Kate Smith) and the audience response to the themes; (3) the congruency of the public images of the figure with the emotional meanings of war bonds; (4) the predispositions of the audience subjected to persuasive appeals; (5) and the social and cultural setting to which the symbolism of appeal and personality traits are attached.

Merton's studies of the reciprocal relation between science and society have required both historical and contemporary settings. In the development of science during the early modern era, Merton is able convincingly to demonstrate the role of such social variables as religious belief (English and American Puritanism and later German Pietism), economic incentives, and technological improvements. Conversely, he examines the strains which science has produced in contemporary society, the generalized loci of conflict between science and modern society, as well as the more specific antagonisms provoked by opposition to the ethics of science and by the social dislocations resulting from the technological applications of science. . . .

To some sociologists, Merton has achieved an unusually successful balance between theory construction and empirical research. Yet Parsons, Becker, MacIver, Znaniecki, and Lundberg have also contended — with varying emphasis — that systematic theory and concrete investigations are mutually required in scientific sociology. Various aspects of conceptual framework are being tested and refined by American sociologists studying bureaucracy, mass communications, intergroup relations, kinship, military life, political movements, professions, religion, social stratification, and small groups. Since this trend is likely to continue, present-day students of sociology will find it advantageous to acquire proficiency in the use of analytical systems of sociological theorists.

## Notes

1. Howard W. Odum, *American Sociology* (New York: Longmans, Green & Co., Inc., 1951), p. 435.

2. Wilfredo Pareto, *Mind and Society*. Trans. and ed. Arthur Livingston, 4 vols. (New York: Harcourt, Brace & Co., 1935). See also the following excellent discussions of Pareto's work: Lawrence J. Henderson, *Pareto's General Sociology* (Cambridge, Mass.: Harvard University Press, 1935); Talcott Parsons, *The Structure of Social Action* (Glencoe, Ill.: The Free Press, 1949), chaps. V, VI, and VII.

3. Emile Durkheim, *The Division of Labor in Society*. Trans. George Simpson (Glencoe, Ill.: The Free Press, 1949); *The Rules of Sociological Method*. Trans. Sarah A. Solovay and John H. Mueller and ed. George E. G. Catlin (Glencoe, Ill.: The Free Press, 1950); *The Elementary Forms of the Religious Life*. Trans. Joseph W. Swain (Glencoe, Ill.: The Free Press, 1947); Harry Alpert, *Emile Durkheim and His Sociology* (New York: Columbia University Press, 1939); Talcott Parsons, *The Structure of Social Action,* chaps. VIII, IX, X, and XI.

4. This concept is found in Emile Durkheim, *Suicide*. Trans. and ed. John A. Spaulding and George Simpson (Glencoe, Ill.: The Free Press, 1951). This book is of interest to sociologists not only for its discussion of the problem of suicide but especially for its research procedures.

5. For a detailed analysis of the history of psychoanalysis in American sociology see: Gisela J. Hinkle, "The Role of Freudianism in American Sociology." (Ph.D. diss., University of Wisconsin, 1951).

6. For a representative selection of Freud's works see Sigmund Freud, *An Outline of Psychoanalysis* (New York: W. W. Norton & Co., Inc., 1949); A. A. Brill, *The Basic Writings of Sigmund Freud* (New York: Modern Library, Inc., 1938). In his *Man in Society: Studies in Sociology* (New York: Random House, Inc., 1954), pp. 39–44, George Simpson has an excellent summary of psychoanalysis and its relevance to sociology.

7. Talcott Parsons, Robert F. Bales, and Edward A. Shils, *Working Papers in the Theory of Action* (Glencoe, Ill.: The Free Press, 1953).

8. Most of Max Weber's major works have now been translated, including *General Economic History*. Trans. Frank H. Knight (London: Allen and Unwin, Ltd., 1927); *The Protestant Ethic and the Spirit of Capitalism*, Trans. Talcott Parsons (London: Allen and Unwin, Ltd., 1930); *The Theory of Social and Economic Organization*, Trans. and ed. Talcott Parsons and A. M. Henderson (New York: Oxford University Press, 1947); *Essays in Sociology,* Trans. and ed. H. H. Gerth and C. W. Mills (New York: Oxford University Press, 1946); *The Methodology of the Social Sciences*. Trans. E. A. Shils and H. A. Finch (Glencoe, Ill.: The Free Press, 1949); *The Religion of China:*

*Confucianism and Taoism*. Trans. H. H. Gerth (Glencoe, Ill.: The Free Press, 1951); *Ancient Judaism*. Trans. H. H. Gerth and Don Martindale (Glencoe, Ill.: The Free Press, 1952).

For summaries of Weber's work see Talcott Parsons, *The Structure of Social Action,* chaps. XIV, XV, XVI, and XVII.

9. For a popular account of this position, see George Lundberg, *Can Science Save Us?* (New York: Longmans, Green & Co., Inc., 1947).

10. This analysis of Lundberg is based on his *Foundations of Sociology* (New York: The Macmillan Co., 1939). The more recent *Sociology*, which was written with Clarence C. Schrag and Otto N. Larsen (New York: Harper & Brothers, 1954), does not seem to indicate any major alterations in Lundberg's own position as here presented. In addition to the two volumes mentioned and *Can Science Save Us?,* Lundberg is the author of *Social Research, A Study in Methods of Gathering Data* (New York: Longmans, Green and Co., Inc., 1942); co-author with Mirra Komarovsky and Mary Alice McInery of *Leisure: A Suburban Study* (New York: Columbia University Press, 1934); and co-editor with Read Bain and Nels Anderson of *Trends in American Sociology* (New York: Harper and Brothers, 1929); and is as well author of numerous articles in sociological and other scientific journals.

11. George A. Lundberg, *Foundations of Sociology* (New York: The Macmillan Co., 1939), pp. 90, 113, and footnotes 4 on pp. 126–127 and 29 on p. 132.

12. For an account of the contemporary methodological dispute between neo-positivism and social action theory, see George Simpson, *Man in Society* (Studies in Sociology) (New York: Random House, Inc., 1954), pp. 48–60.

13. The following and Znaniecki's principal publications in English: *Cultural Reality* (Chicago: University of Chicago Press, 1919); *The Laws of Social Psychology* (Chicago: University of Chicago Press, 1925); *The Method of Sociology* (New York: Farrar & Rinehart, Inc., 1934); *Social Actions* (New York: Farrar & Rinehart, Inc., 1936); *The Social Role of the Man of Knowledge* (New York: Columbia University Press, 1940); *Modern Nationalities, a Sociological Study* (Urbana, Ill.: University of Illinois, 1952); *Cultural Sciences, Their Origin and Development* (Urbana, Ill.: University of Illinois, 1952); and William I. Thomas and Florian Znaniecki, *The Polish Peasant in Europe and America,* 5 vols. (Chicago: University of Chicago Press, 1918–1920).

14. MacIver is the author of *Labor in the Changing World* (New York: E. P. Dutton and Co., 1919); *The Modern State* (London: H. Milford, Oxford University Press, 1928); *The Contributions of Sociology to Social Work* (New York: Columbia University, 1931); *Leviathan and the People* (University Station, Baton Rouge, La.: Louisiana State University Press, 1939); *Social Causation* (New York: Ginn & Co., 1942); *Towards an Abiding Peace* (New

York: The Macmillan Co., 1943); *The Web of Government* (New York: The Macmillan Co., 1947); *The More Perfect Union* (New York: The Macmillan Co., 1948); *The Ramparts We Guard* (New York: The Macmillan Co., 1950); *Democracy and Economic Challenge* (New York: Alfred A. Knopf, Inc., 1952). He is co-author with Moritz J. Bonn and Ralph Barton Perry of *The Roots of Totalitarianism* (Philadelphia: The American Academy of Political and Social Science, 1940), and with Charles H. Page of *Society: An Introductory Analysis* (New York: Rinehart & Co., Inc., 1949). He was editor of *Group Relations and Group Antagonisms*, 1944; *Civilization and Group Relationships*, 1945; *Unity and Difference in American Life*, 1947; *Discrimination and National Welfare*, 1949; *Great Expressions of Human Rights*, 1950; *Conflict of Loyalties*, 1952; all published in New York by Harper & Brothers for the Institute for Religious and Social Studies.

15. Becker's major publications include the following: Wiese-Becker: *Systematic Sociology* (New York: John Wiley & Sons, Inc., 1932); Harry Elmer Barnes and Howard Becker: *Social Thought from Lore to Science*, 2 vols. (Boston: D. C. Heath & Co., 1938); Howard Becker, *German Youth: Bond or Free* (London: K. Paul, Trench, Trubner and Co., Ltd., 1946); Harry E. Barnes, Howard Becker, and Frances B. Becker: *Contemporary Social Theory* (New York: D. Appleton-Century Co., Inc., 1940); Howard Becker and Reuben Hill, eds.: *Family, Marriage and Parenthood* (Boston: D. C. Heath & Co., 1948); Howard Becker, *Through Values to Social Interpretation* (Durham, N.C.: Duke University Press, 1950).

16. See his *Essays in Sociological Theory* (Glencoe, Ill.: The Free Press, 1949).

17. His *The Social System* (Glencoe, Ill.: The Free Press, 1951), should be read in conjunction with Talcott Parsons and Edward A. Shils, eds., *Toward a General Theory of Action* (Cambridge, Mass.: Harvard University Press, 1951), and Talcott Parsons, Robert F. Bales, and Edward A. Shils: *Working Papers in the Theory of Action* (Glencoe, Ill.: The Free Press, 1953). These volumes were preceded by Parsons' *The Structure of Social Action* (1937), a second printing of which was issued by The Free Press, 1949).

18. William J. Goode and Paul K. Hatt, *Methods in Social Research* (New York: McGraw-Hill Book Co., Inc., 1952) note pages 9–16 that theory and fact have reciprocal roles in the scientific method. Their conception of this reciprocity follows Merton's own view in *Social Theory and Social Structure* (Glencoe, Ill: The Free Press, 1949), pp. 83–96 and pp. 97–111.

19. Robert K. Merton, *Social Theory and Social Structure* (Glencoe, Ill.: The Free Press, 1949), pp. 50–54.

20. For illuminating illustrations of this and other functionalist concepts, see Ely Chinoy, *Sociological Perspective* (Studies in Sociology) (New York: Random House, Inc., 1954), pp. 37–47.

21. Merton, *Social Theory*. See also Robert K. Merton, Marjorie Fiske, and Alberta Curtis, *Mass Persuasion* (New York: Harper & Brothers, 1946);

Robert K. Merton, Marjorie Fiske, and Patricia Kendall, *The Focussed Interview,* 2nd ed. (New York: Bureau of Applied Social Research, Columbia University, 1952). Merton is also editor, with Paul F. Lazarsfeld, of *Continuities in Social Research* (Glencoe, Ill.: The Free Press, 1950), and with Ailsa P. Gray, Barbara Hockey, and Hahan C. Selvin of *Reader in Bureaucracy* (Glencoe, Ill.: The Free Press, 1952).

# 13

# Conclusion

In the preceding pages we have presented the developmental thread that runs from social philosophy to modern sociology. That thread changes in hue and texture as it runs from divergent philosophical orientations toward a more cohesive body of theory. In the effort to relate the origins and growth of sociological theory a process of selectivity has naturally taken place. The authors and ideas discussed in this volume represent a necessarily limited view of the entire body of work from which the selections were made. It is our sincere feeling that a fair and reasonable presentation has been made.

As is true of most things in our present-day world, sociology has become increasingly complex. That complexity and diversity is evident in sociological theory. No one theory or school of theory has ever enjoyed absolute dominance in sociology — a healthy, if somewhat disconcerting situation. The mosaic of human interactive life, reflected in the variegated systems of social organizations that have occurred, has allowed, indeed fostered, many viable theoretical perspectives concerned with the behavior of human beings in groups. Perhaps the one school of theory that has come closest to an overriding dominance in sociology has been "sociological functionalism."

Sociological functionalism has been traced back to the works of the cultural anthropologists A. R. Radcliffe-Brown and Bronislaw Malinowsky. The growth and general acceptance of functionalism (structuralism) in anthropology contributed to its adoption in sociology. Although arguments may arise as to the genesis of functionalism there is little argument as to who has been the dominant proponent of it. Talcott Parsons (b. 1902) in *The Social System*[1] established himself as the foremost proponent of the functionalist perspective. The success and acceptance of this, and subsequent work of Parsons, as well as the significant contributions of others, brought a preeminence to sociological functionalism that remained unchallenged for more than a decade. There is not complete agreement as to the appropriateness of characterizing Parsons' theory after 1951 as being a complete departure from his previous social-action orientation. It has been argued that Parsons' latter orientation is merely an extension or reinforcement of his previous work. Others, of course, view the functionalist perspective as being a significant new direction in sociological theory.

Simply stated, functionalism treats social action as being structured into social, personality, and cultural systems. For Parsons, "structural-functional" analysis requires systematic treatment of the statuses and roles of actors in a social situation as well as the institutional patterns involved. A central concern in the work of Parsons and other functionalists has been the question of the functional requirements that must be met by any social system if it is to survive.

Another theory that developed simultaneously with functionalism was Pitirim Sorokin's (1889–1968) "integralist school." This school studies social phenomena in three ways:

1. In their empirical aspect, through sense perception
2. In their logico-rational aspect, through discursive logic of human reason
3. In their supersensory, superrational, metalogical aspect, through the truth of faith (supersensory, superrational, metalogical act of intuition or mystic experience)

A third theory enjoying wide acceptance is "symbolic interactionism." It began with G. Mead (1863–1931) and C. Cooley (1864–1929) of the Chicago School of Social Psychology. One of the leading proponents of symbolic interactionism is H. Blumer (b. 1900) who emphasizes that human interaction is a positive shaping process in its own right and that human group life takes on the character of an ongoing process. He believes that the actors have to judge the fitness of norms, values, and group prescriptions, and that social control is a matter of self-control.

A fourth perspective in contemporary sociology, gaining notice during the 1950s due to its strong criticism of Parsonian functionalism, is "conflict theory." Conflict theories find their inspiration either in the works of Marx (dialectical conflict theories) or Simmel (conflict functionalism.). Conflict theories in sociology — as opposed to functional theory — view conflict as a natural and inevitable aspect of the social system. More recently, however, some authors point to areas of reconciliation between the two perspectives, and claim that a synthesis of the divergent views of functionalism and conflict theory is possible.[2]

Finally, a theory that is still trying to gain general acceptance in sociological circles is "ethnomethodology." This theory is defined as "the study of the methods used by members of a group for understanding communications, making decisions, being rational, accounting for action, and so on." The implications of ethnomethodology are rather revolutionary, but the future of this new perspective in sociology is still uncertain. Some sociologists expect that ethnomethodology will be absorbed into traditional sociology; others believe that ethnomethodology will become an independent discipline; finally, a few others foresee a gradual disappearance of ethnomethodology in the near future.

In addition to the various theoretical perspectives that exist in present-day sociology an over-all dichotomy of opinion exists as to what *sociologists* should or should not be. Our discussion in this volume, and those of other writers that appear here, have been primarily concerned with the theoretical development of the discipline of sociology. Although individual sociologists are obviously responsible for the ideas presented, little consideration has been given here to the role of the sociologist per se. It is a question that can easily engender heated debate whenever sociologists gather. The basic division is between those sociologists who believe in a "value-free" sociology, and those who opt for a "value-committed" sociology. Other labels for these two orientations are often used. Some prefer the terms "prescriptive/nonprescriptive"; others prefer "objective/subjective." Whatever terminology is used, it is obvious that there exists a legitimate and serious concern about what sociologists and sociology should be. After World War I American sociologists became more conscious of the need to deal inductively with empirical phenomena, and since then the objectivist/subjectivist conflict has divided American sociology.

Timasheff and Theodorson address the more general formulation of this problem, which they label "the value dilemma."[3] They call attention to the fact that there are increasing objections to the value-free "objective" character of sociology, as well as increasing demands that sociology become "value-committed." Three major methods of dealing with this dilemma are offered. One possible resolution is "the systematic integration of sociology with the scholarly tradition of moral philosophy."[4] Another alternative suggests "the abandonment of an attempt . . . at scientific objectivity, but, unlike the first alternative, does not advocate a systematic integration of sociology with moral philosophy."[5] The third alternative, according to Timasheff and Theodorson, holds the most promise for sociology. According to them, proponents of this view "accept objectivity as an ideal fundamental to modern science itself and therefore always to be approximated as closely as possible."[6] In other words, it should be recognized that sociology, as a science, requires the same attention to objectivity found in other sciences. At the same time it must also be recognized that perfect objectivity is probably an unreachable goal. Even the physical sciences, often characterized as being value-free, are in truth less than totally successful in living up to that ideal. It has often been argued that in the physical sciences subjectivity is present. In the act of deciding what problem, relationships, reactions, etc., should be studied, the physical scientist is bringing his or her values to that decision. The result of this fact could well be that many important areas of inquiry are ignored or postponed. Each individual scientist, regardless of his or her area of expertise, possesses a social, cultural, and intellectual identity that may predispose decisions one way or another. Since the "thing" the sociologist studies is the behavior of human beings in groups, the problem of predisposition may be, or at least appears to be, more acute.

The work of C. Wright Mills (1916–1962) provides an excellent example of value-committed sociology. His most familiar work, *The Power Elite,* contains the clear orientation Mills had toward ameliorative sociology.[7] In that work, Mills presents his view of the power structure in the United States. In his view, power is concentrated in the hands of the "big three." The "big three" are the political, economic, and military elites who increasingly control the lives and futures of the bulk of the population. Mills treats these elites as being the primary institutions in our society. He says of them:

> Other institutions seem off to the side of modern history, and, on occasion, duly subordinated to these (big three). No family is as directly powerful in national affairs as any major corporation; no church is as directly powerful in the external biographies of young men in America today as the military establishment; no college is as powerful in the shaping of momentous events as the National Security Council. Religious, educational, and family institutions are not autonomous centers of national power; on the contrary, these de-centralized areas are increasingly shaped by the Big Three, in which developments of decisive and immediate consequences occur.[8]

Mills views the power configuration he has outlined as being detrimental to the democratic principles embodied in the United States. His value orientation leads him to characterize the "reality" of the power elite as being inimical to those principles. He then goes on to outline a plan for the rectification of the situation. An example of Mills' tilt toward prescriptive sociology is related by Irving L. Horowitz, a disciple of Mills: "As Mills once said in a letter to a 'white-collar wife' published in a weekly mass circulation publication, 'It is one thing to talk about general problems on a national level, and quite another to tell an individual what to do. Most "experts" dodge that question. I do not want to.' "[9]

Our discussion of the "value-dilemma" would not be complete without mentioning still another division that is present in sociology. It is a division that runs a course somewhat parallel to the "value-free–value-committed" division. It is concerned with the *doing* of sociology — the type of methodology to be utilized in sociological investigation and explanation. The basic division finds those who prefer empirical or quantitative methodology on one side, and those who prefer qualitative methodology on the other.

Quantitative sociological methodology employs the strict rigors of empirical science. The analysis of the relationship of variables is usually carried out through some type of statistical testing. According to James S. Coleman "the mathematics which is necessary in such work requires first of all quantitative measurement of the concepts."[10] The problem then is to arrive at a satisfactory quantitative measurement of variables such as social cohesion, attitudes on various behaviors, etc. This problem, in the minds of some, seriously delimits the application of quantitative methods.

Qualitative sociological methodology is less easily defined than is quantitative methodology. Perhaps the best way to describe it is to use Max Weber's concept of *verstehen*. *Verstehen*, usually defined as "interpretive understanding," requires that the sociologist immerse himself or herself in the study of a particular behavior in order to understand the inner feelings, motivations, etc., that produced the behavior.

It should be pointed out that the two methodologies briefly recounted here are not mutually exclusive. In actual practice they can be and often are, combined. The labels of "quantitative" or "qualitative" simply allude to an individual's primary orientation. That orientation may or may not be totally determinative as to the way a sociological study is carried out.

The interplay between theory and methodology is intricate. In fact, it is by itself a significant area of sociological study. It is mentioned in this volume to show the student the diverse threads that compose the fabric that we know as the discipline of sociology. It is hoped that the inclusion will serve to sensitize interested students to the nuances at work in the writings they have just completed studying.

The study of the origins and growth of sociological theory provides the student with some sense of the developmental process present in any area of intellectual endeavor. From Auguste Comte to the present we have witnessed the refinement and specialization occurring in the study of the behavior of human beings in groups. Some of the thinkers represented in this work have had a widespread, significant impact on the world we live in today. The influence of others has been more limited. However, all of those thinkers presented in this work have helped to produce sociological theory as it exists today.

The criticisms of the past decade have contributed to point out unwarranted assumptions, weaknesses and other shortcomings in sociological theories. Yet, they did not prevent sociologists from reaching basic agreements on many substantial areas. Let us conclude our historical view of the origins and growth of sociological theory with the following final remark of Timasheff and Theodorson: "We may anticipate that the future of sociology will see the continual modification of current approaches, as well as the emergence of new perspectives, and the rediscovery and revival of long-standing orientations in new and interesting combinations. We may also expect sociological theory to be influenced, as it has been in the past, by developments in other disciplines, such as philosophy, physics, economics, and so forth. Disagreements, and heated debates will no doubt continue to flourish. Each of us, as students of society, should participate in this ferment. With an understanding of the heritage of the past and the alternatives of the present, we can work toward greater theoretical synthesis and a better understanding of social phenomena."[11]

## Notes

1. Talcott Parsons, *The Social System* (Glencoe, Ill.: The Free Press, 1951).
2. See Pierre L. Van Den Berghe, "Dialectic and Functionalism: Toward a Theoretical Synthesis," *American Sociological Review* (October 1963), pp. 695–705.
3. Nicholas S. Timasheff and George A. Theodorson, *Sociological Theory, Its Nature and Growth,* 4th ed. (New York: Random House, 1976), p. 358.

4. Ibid., p. 358.
5. Ibid., p. 358.
6. Ibid., p. 359.
7. C. Wright Mills, *The Power Elite* (New York: Oxford University Press, 1956).
8. Ibid., p. 6.
9. Irving L. Horowitz, ed., *C. Wright Mills — Power, Politics, and People,* (New York: Ballantine Books, 1963).
10. James S. Coleman, in R. E. L. Faris, ed., *Handbook of Modern Sociology,* (Chicago: Rand McNally and Co., 1964), p. 1,028.
11. Timasheff and Theodorson, *Sociological Theory,* p. 361.

# INDEX

193